The Improv Seri[es]
BLUES SOLOING STRATEGIE[S]

MW01040504

Concepts for Various Blues Styles
WAYNE RIKER

*Alfred, the leader in educational music publishing,
and the National Guitar Workshop,
one of America's finest guitar schools, have joined
forces to bring you the best, most progressive
educational tools possible. We hope you will enjoy
this book and encourage you to look for
other fine products from Alfred and the
National Guitar Workshop.*

This book was acquired, edited, and produced
by Workshop Arts, Inc., the publishing arm of
the National Guitar Workshop.
Nathaniel Gunod, acquisitions, managing editor
Burgess Speed, acquisitions, senior editor
Timothy Phelps, interior design
Ante Gelo, music typesetter
CD recorded at Studio 9, Pomona, CA

Alfred Music Publishing Co., Inc.
P.O. Box 10003
Van Nuys, CA 91410-0003
alfred.com

ISBN-10: 0-7390-8253-1 (Book & CD)
ISBN-13: 978-0-7390-8253-9 (Book & CD)

CONTENTS

A compact disc is included with this book. Using the CD will help make learning more enjoyable and the information more meaningful. The symbol below appears at the top of the first page of every solo. It will help you find the track on the CD.

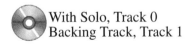

With Solo, Track 0
Backing Track, Track 1

The CD provides recordings of the author performing the solos in this book and backing tracks for you to practice with. Track 1 will help you tune to the CD.

For the sake of musicality, an intro has been added to each solo on the CD. The solo as transcribed in the book begins several bars into each track.

ABOUT THE AUTHOR

Wayne Riker has been a guitar teacher and performer since 1970, playing and teaching all styles of music. A graduate of the Guitar Institute of Technology (1980), Wayne was a senior faculty member of the National Guitar Workshop (1990–2006), conducting and co-hosting blues workshops at most of the NGW campuses, in addition to writing instructional columns for *Guitar Player, Acoustic Guitar,* and *Premier Guitar* magazines. Currently, he is a freelance guitarist and composer in the San Diego area, recording original instrumental tracks with his quintet, as well as solo acoustic guitar material. His two recent CDs, *Fretology* and *Penumbral Sky,* have received high acclaim.

For updates and contact information, please visit: www.waynerikerguitar.com

PHOTO BY DENNIS ANDERSEN

Dedication

This book is dedicated to the people of my hometown, New York City, post 9–11–01.

Other Books by Wayne Riker

> *Mastering Blues Guitar* (Alfred/NGW #8234)
>
> *Blues Guitar: Complete Edition,* with David Hamburger and Matt Smith (Alfred/NGW #34349)
>
> *No Reading Required: Easy Blues Guitar Licks,* DVD (Alfred/NGW #23225)
>
> *Blues Licks Encyclopedia* (Alfred #18503)
>
> *Guitar Roots: Chicago Blues* (Alfred #18483)
>
> The Slide chapter in *The Guitar Technique Encyclopedia* (Alfred #19381)

INTRODUCTION

Welcome to *Blues Soloing Strategies for Guitar*. This book, which is intended for intermediate guitarists, provides a great opportunity for you to learn how to better structure and shape a blues solo by studying 8- and 12-bar solos in a variety of keys. Some of these solos extend through two and three choruses, creating 16-, 24- and 36-bar scenarios. In solos with more than one chorus, the end of each chorus is marked with a double bar. Eleven blues solo styles, including Chicago, Delta, rock, slow, "Stormy Monday," minor, funk, jump, jazz, and gospel, are analyzed harmonically, rhythmically, and melodically to help you learn to create a strong musical solo. Make sure to use the accompanying CD to hear the rhythmic feel, tempo, and chord voicings for each example. The CD also includes a backing track for each solo, allowing you to practice jamming along with the band. At the back of the book there is a scale glossary and an arpeggio glossary as references for many of the licks used in these solos and for creating your own.

To get the most out of this book, you should already be familiar with:

- Reading standard music notation and/or tablature
- Scales: major, minor, pentatonic, and the modes of the major scale
- Blues techniques such as bending, slides, vibrato, and so on
- Music theory, including chord construction and diatonic harmony (using Roman numerals to describe chord progressions, such as I–IV–V)
- Chord extensions and alterations, such C9 or C7$\sharp$9
- The most basic blues form, the 12-bar blues

There is a quick review of reading standard music notation and tablature in the following four pages (6–9). For basic information about music theory, check out any or all of the following books from the National Guitar Workshop and Alfred:

Beginning Blues and Rock Theory for Guitar (Alfred #21962)
Beginning Blues Guitar (Alfred #8230)
Intermediate Blues Guitar (Alfred #8233)
Theory for the Contemporary Guitarist (Alfred #16755)

Creating a solo is like writing a story. You want to present a thoughtful beginning, middle, and end to tell a tale that will capture the audience's attention. Many of these solos are compilations of ideas I've generated by listening to players in all styles of music. As you compile your own vocabulary of licks, make sure you are always aware of what chord the lick is being used against. A lick that works well on the I chord may not work as well over the V chord, and so on.

Apply the ideas in this book along with information from other sources, such as the *Blues Licks Encyclopedia* (Alfred #18503). If you haven't already, start playing with other musicians. Learning to play strong, musical solos is difficult unless you jam with other musicians and hear the dynamics of your solo in a group setting. Jam with a friend, join a group, attend jam sessions, or play along with backing tracks.

Enjoy!

Wayne Riker

READING STANDARD MUSIC NOTATION AND TABLATURE (TAB) —A QUICK REVIEW

Knowing how to read music will help you to get the most out of this book. It will make you a better musician, too, because you will be able to communicate more easily with other musicians. What follows is a quick review of music-reading basics. If you don't need it, feel free to skip it. Remember that practice makes perfect! The more you practice reading, the easier it will become.

Pitch

The Staff and Notes

Music is written on a *staff* containing five lines and four spaces. Notes are written on the lines and spaces to tell us which *pitches* (degrees of highness or lowness) to play.

Clef

The *clef* indicates which notes coincide with a particular line or space. Different clefs are used for different instruments. Guitar music is written in the *G clef*. The inside curl of the G clef encircles the line that is called "G." When the G clef is placed on the second line, as in guitar music, it is called the *treble clef*.

When using the G clef, the notes are as follows:*

Ledger Lines

Ledger lines are used to indicate pitches above and below the staff.

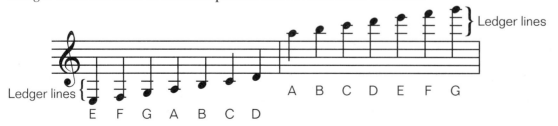

* In standard notation, the guitar sounds an *octave* (12 frets) lower than written.

Time

Measures and Bar Lines

The staff is divided by vertical lines called *bar lines*. The space between two bar lines is a *measure,* or *bar*. Each measure (bar) is an equal unit of time.

Double bar lines mark the end of a section or example.

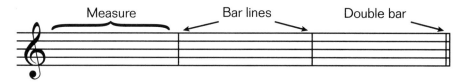

Note and Rest Values

When silence is required, a *rest* symbol is used. The diagrams below show the note and rest values and their relationships to one another.

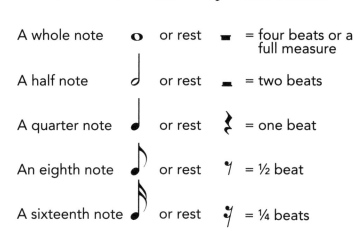

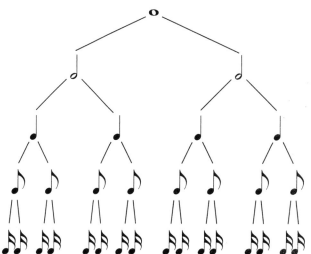

Time Signature

Every piece of music has numbers at the beginning called a *time signature* that tell us how to count the time. The top number represents the number of beats or counts per measure. The bottom number represents the type of note receiving one count. For example:

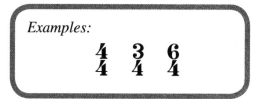

Examples:
$$\frac{4}{4} \quad \frac{3}{4} \quad \frac{6}{4}$$

Consecutive notes shorter than a quarter note are usually *beamed* together in groups.

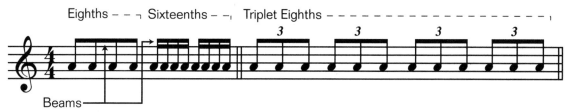

Triplets

Blues rhythms, at their core, are based on a "three" feel. This particular effect comes from dividing each beat (quarter note) into three equal parts, creating an *eighth-note triplet* rhythm. Try clapping the following triplet rhythm, counting along as you clap: 1–&–a, 2–&–a, 3–&–a, 4–&–a.

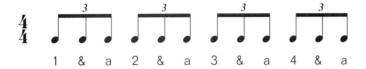

Swing 8ths

Almost all blues songs use a rhythmic pattern called *swing eighths,* or *shuffle rhythm.* Swing eighths are normally written like even eighth notes but sound something like a triplet group in which the first two triplets are tied together. Grooves or tunes that use this rhythmic pattern are often called *shuffles.*

In this book, solos that are played with a swing feel are marked *Swing 8ths.* All other solos, with no *Swing 8ths* indication, are played with regular, straight eighth notes.

Tablature (TAB)

The combination of *tablature* (TAB) and standard music notation provides the most complete system for communicating the many possibilities in guitar playing.

Six lines are used to indicate the six strings of the guitar. The top line is the 1st, high E string (the thinnest string, closest to the floor) and the bottom line is the 6th, low E string (the thickest string, closest to the ceiling). Numbers are placed on the strings to indicate frets. If there is a "0," play that string open. In the TAB used in this book, rhythm is not indicated. For that, you will have to refer to the standard music notation above the TAB.

Fingerings are often included in TAB. You will find them just under the bottom line. (The fingers of the left hand are numbered 1 through 4, starting with the index finger.)

In the following example, the first note is played with the 1st finger on the 1st fret. The next note is played with the 2nd finger on the 2nd fret, the 3rd finger plays the 3rd fret, and the 4th finger plays the 4th fret, all on the 1st string.

A *tie* in the music (a curved line that joins two or more notes of the same pitch into one longer note) is indicated in TAB by placing the tied note in parentheses.

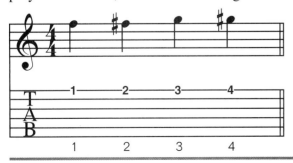

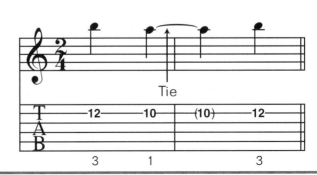

Hammer-ons (sounding a note with just the left hand) and *pull-offs* (pulling a left-hand finger off a string in such a way as to sound a note without plucking with the right hand) are indicated with *slur* marks, just as in standard notation. We also use "H" for hammer-ons and "P" for pull-offs. These are found just above the TAB.

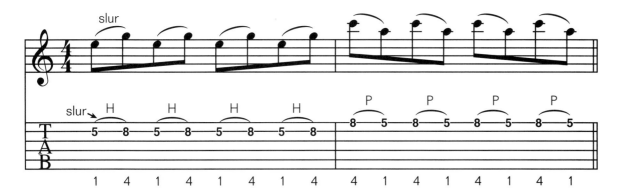

Upward bends are marked with upward arrows. Downward arrows are used to show a bend being released. A number above the arrow indicates how far to bend (1 = a whole step, ½ = a half step, etc.). Remember that the TAB will show the fret number on which your finger should be placed. The standard music notation shows the actual resulting sound. Notice that the small *grace note* in the standard notation corresponds with the fret shown in the TAB. In the following example, you will also find a *tap* (T) and a *slide* (S and ⟋). Also, notice that the fret number of a released bend is in parentheses. Some notes are actually represented by the arrows themselves, as in the second note of the triplet in the TAB of this example.

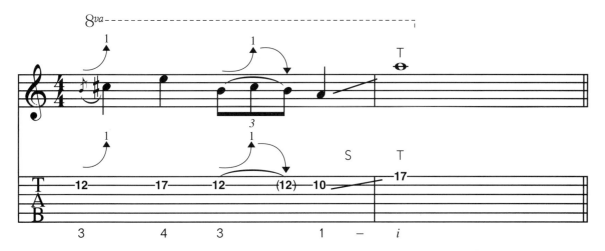

In the following example, you will find several more symbols used in TAB: the sign for *vibrato* (〰), and the signs for picking down (⊓) and the sign for picking up (Ⅴ).

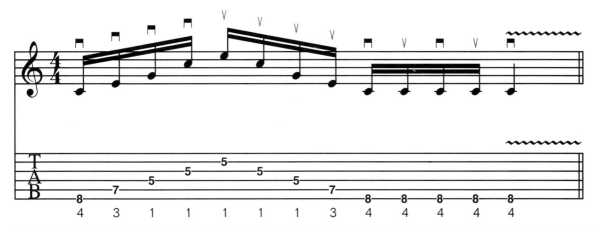

CHICAGO BLUES

This solo is in a 12-bar shuffle-style Chicago blues that covers two choruses. It is in the very guitar-friendly key of E.

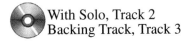 With Solo, Track 2
Backing Track, Track 3

Chicago Blues Shuffle

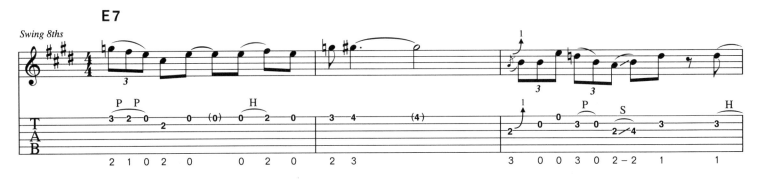

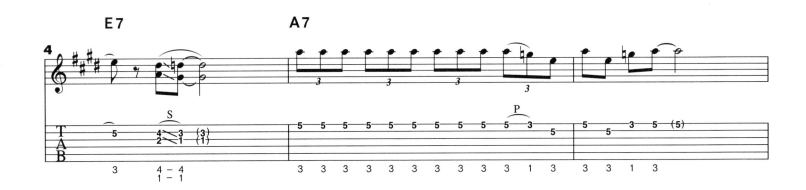

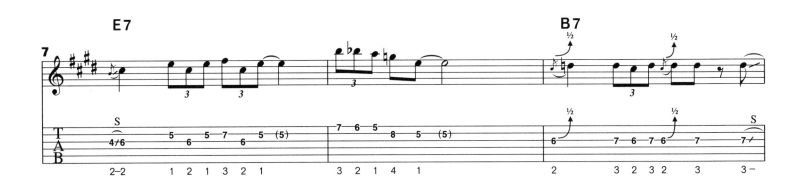

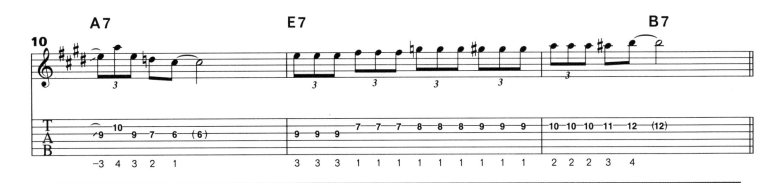

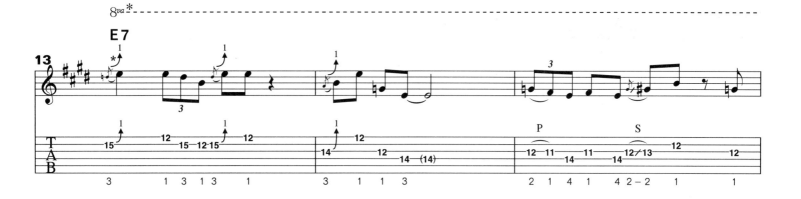

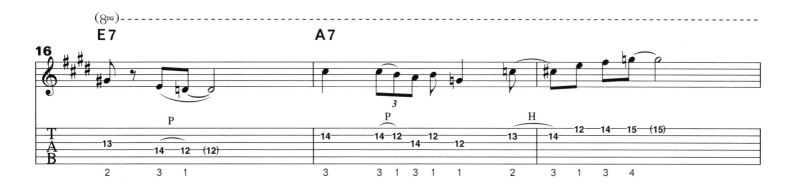

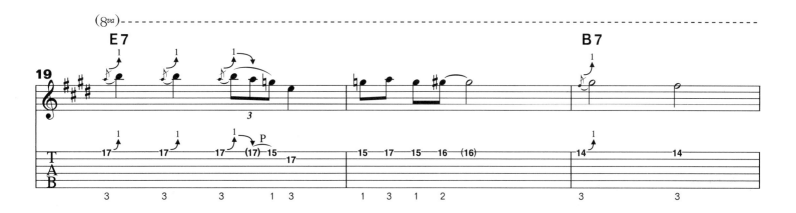

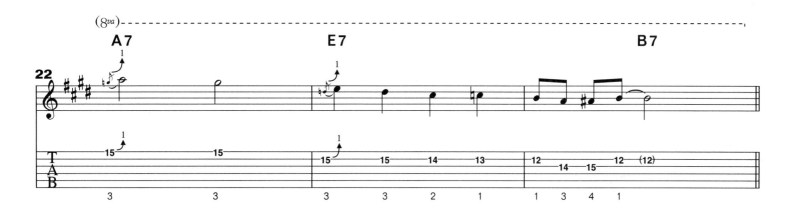

* = *Ottava Alta.* Play an octave higher than written.

Analysis

A great way to structure a solo over two back-to-back choruses is to start the first chorus in *open position* (the open strings and first four frets) and then proceed gradually up the fretboard into the higher positions. **Bars 1–4** employ a combination of the E Major Pentatonic and E Minor Pentatonic scales (see page 94 for a glossary of scales).

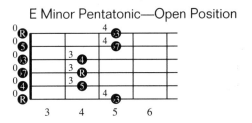

E Minor Pentatonic—Open Position

A blend of these two scales is a potent combination for shaping a blues solo. The major pentatonic scale highlights the root (E), major 3rd (G♯), 5th (B), 6th (C♯), and 9th (F♯) of the chord. The minor pentatonic scale accents some of the characteristic *blue notes* (tones that clearly convey the blues character), specifically the ♭3rd (G) and the ♭7th (D). Notice the use of hammer-ons, pull-offs, slides, and bends to make the licks more expressive. The effective use of *double stops* (two notes played simultaneously by a single player) in **bar 4** accentuates the chord tones G♯ and D, the 3rd and ♭7th, respectively, demanding a strong resolution to the IV chord in **bar 5**.

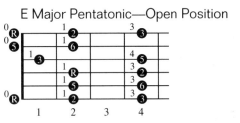

E Major Pentatonic—Open Position

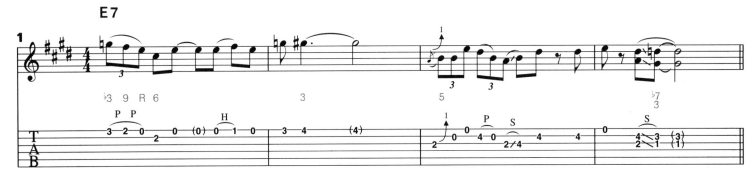

In **bar 5**, the use of a repetitive triplet figure is a slick way to drive the solo rhythmically, while supporting the harmony by emphasizing the root (A) of the IV chord.

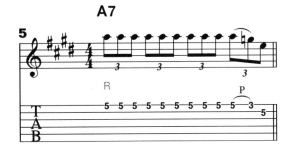

Contrasting the E Major Pentatonic and E Minor Pentatonic scales in **bars 7–8**, respectively, and the resulting combination of scale tones, continues to add color to the solo. The scale tones are labeled in gray the first time they occur.

At **bar 9**, the solo aims specifically at a pair of tones over the V chord (B7). The use of the 9th and the ♭3rd, both important *color tones* in blues, makes a solid argument for quality over quantity of notes in a blues solo. Color tones are generally tones that lend a special flavor to the chord, such as the 9th. Playing simple motifs over the V chord that accent important colors is a powerful way to shape a blues solo. In this case, the use of the ♭3rd (D♮) over the unaltered 3rd (D♯) of the dominant chord is an unmistakably bluesy effect.

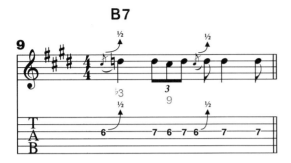

Bar 10 emphasizes the root (A), the 5th (E), and the 3rd (C♯) of the IV chord (A7).

In the *turnaround* (typically, the final bars of a 12-bar blues that are used to bring the tune back to the beginning in a smooth, logical way, most often by ending on the V chord), **bar 11** has a classic ascending lick from the root (E) up to the 3rd (G♯) driven by an eighth-note triplet figure that powers the first chorus to an end.

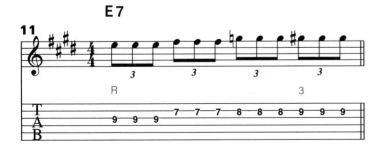

As the second chorus begins in **bar 13**, the immediate move to the upper register establishes an emotional intensity that fuels the solo. Notice the continued bending technique, which keeps the solo bluesy.

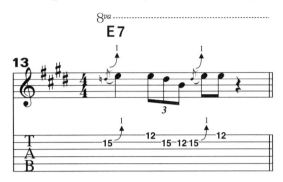

In **bars 15–16**, the pull-offs and slides add expression. The solo shifts from the E Minor Pentatonic scale to the E *Mixolydian mode* (E–F♯–G♯–A–B–C♯–D). The Mixolydian mode is the fifth mode of the major scale, so E Mixolydian has the same notes as an A Major scale although it begins and ends on E. It can also be thought of as a major scale with a ♭7. Using the Mixolydian mode offers some nice melodic alternatives to the minor pentatonic scale by adding the 2nd/9th (F♯), 3rd (G♯), and 6th (C♯) (the 6th is not used in this passage).

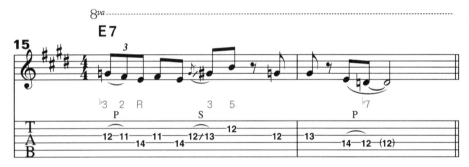

In **bar 17**, notice the strong statement of the 3rd (C♯) of the IV chord (A7). The lick ends on the "&" of beat 2 in **bar 18** on a G, the ♭7th of A7.

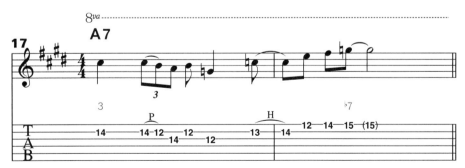

At **bar 19**, notice the consecutive bends to the 5th (B) at the beginning of this short minor pentatonic lick that ends on the root (E).

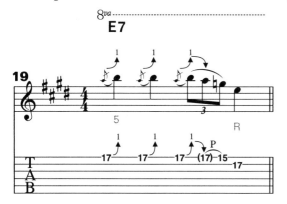

At this point in the solo, quality over quantity of notes becomes imperative. The screaming notes higher up the neck tend to build the solo to a frenzied conclusion. **Bar 20** concludes with a strong punctuation on the G♯, the 3rd of the I chord (E7). Ending a lick with the 3rd is a good way give the phrase some personality.

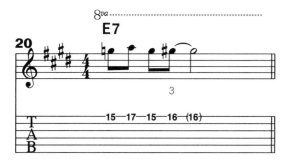

Bars 21–22 simply outline the remaining chords in a basic half-note sequence. This technique acts as a lull after the storm of the previous eight bars and is a great way to shape a solo as it winds down during the turnaround.

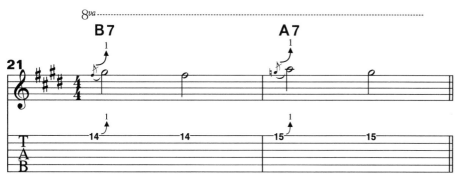

This solo is a three-chorus 12-bar Chicago blues in G.

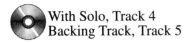
With Solo, Track 4
Backing Track, Track 5

Three Nights in Chicago

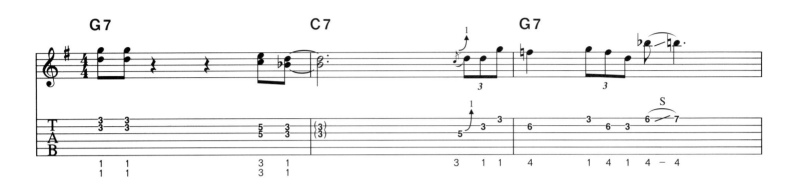

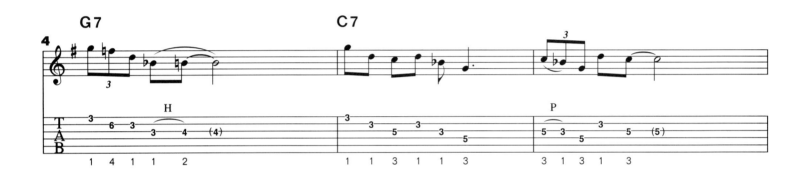

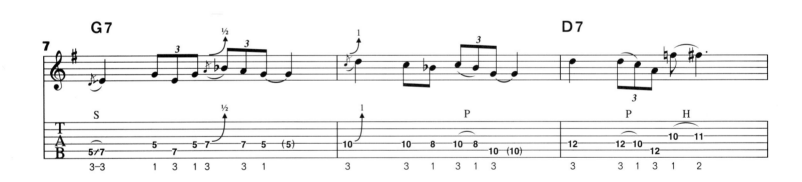

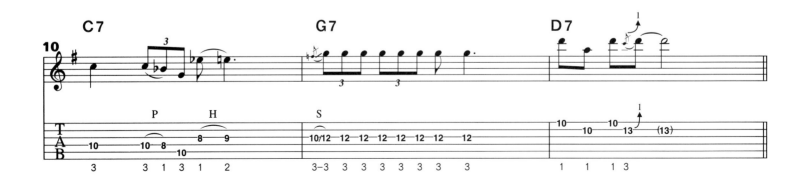

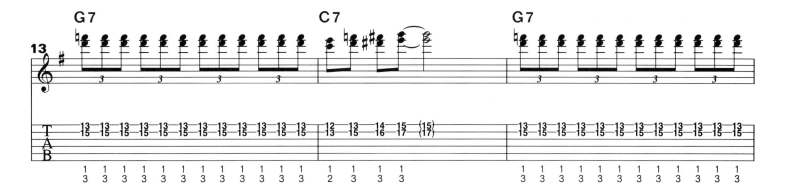

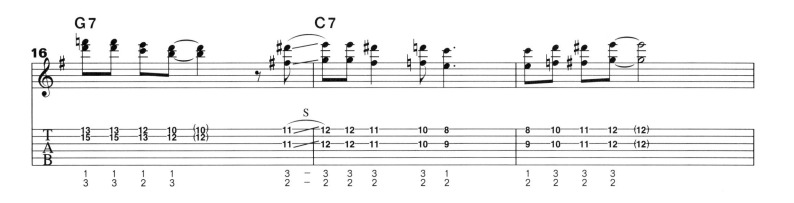

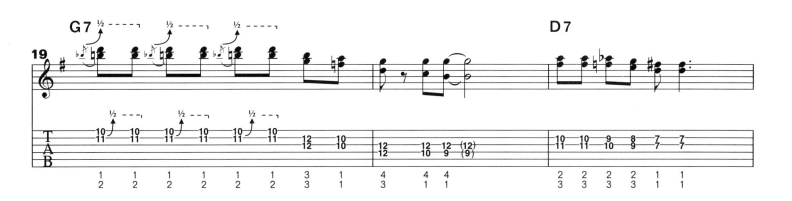

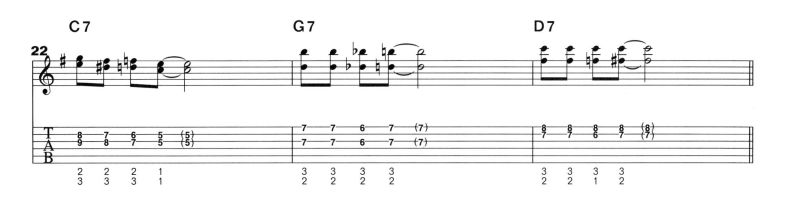

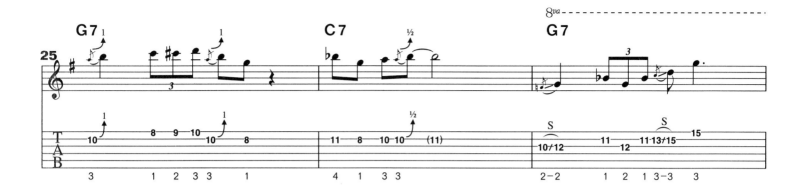

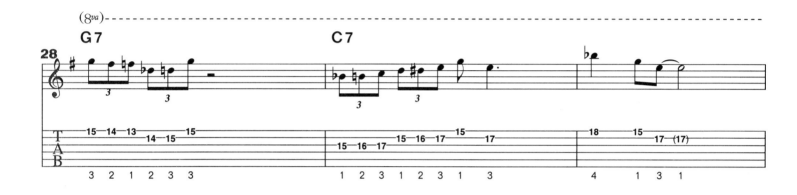

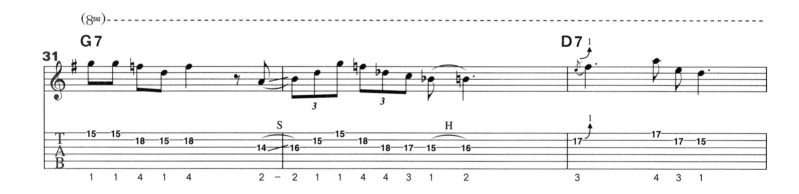

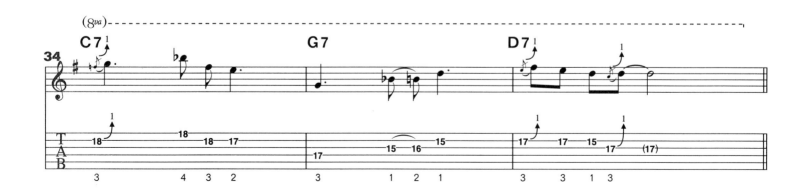

Analysis

An economical way to begin a three-chorus solo is with a simple and concise double-stop lick. If you start the first couple of bars with a multitude of notes, the solo becomes too busy, and generally there is too much intensity too soon.

In **bar 3**, the lick starts on a basic four-note pattern from the G Minor Pentatonic scale (G–B♭–C–D–F) and ends with a slide into the 3rd (B) of the G7 chord. Ending a phrase on a ♮3rd—especially after focusing on the ♭3rd—always strengthens the personality of the solo.

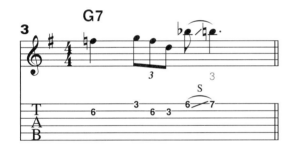
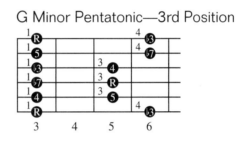

Notice the continued use of the G Minor Pentatonic scale in **bar 5**. Here, the tones of the IV chord (C7) are more pronounced—especially the 5th (G), the ♭7th (B♭), and the root (C). The use of the 9th (D) is also colorful against the C7. Defining these chord tones, thus making meaningful note choices, helps make each note more special. This allows you to play fewer notes. In blues, less is often more.

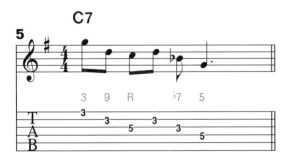

In **bar 7**, the solo moves into a lower register. This is a nice way to break up a solo. Playing only in one register can be monotonous.

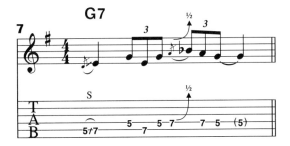

The phrase steadily ascends to the last note of **bar 9**—the F♯, which is the 3rd of the V chord (D7). Ending with a chord tone in this bar is a good idea, because this is the pinnacle of the solo as it approaches the turnaround.

The continued use of pull-offs and hammer-ons in **bar 10** keep the solo expressive. The last note of the bar parallels **bar 9** by finishing on the 3rd (E) of the IV chord (C7).

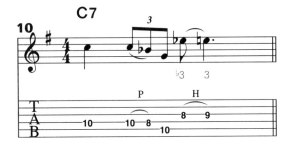

The entire second chorus is played with double stops, which is a good contrast to the first chorus, which is mostly single notes. The double-stop 3rds in **bars 13–14** outline the chord progression nicely. **Bar 13** has chord tones from G7, and **bar 14** moves chromatically from C7 chord tones on the downbeat to chord tones on the "&" of "2."

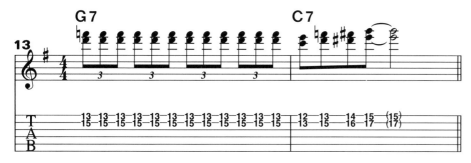

In **bar 17**, the interval combination in the double stops changes to harmonic 6ths. This is another strong way to structure a double-stop solo, because you can still outline the chords, but with a more open sound.

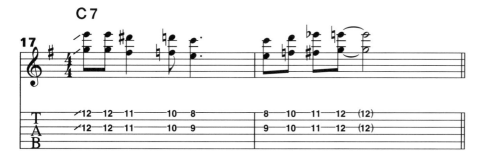

In **bars 21–22**, the double-stop 3rds move *chromatically* (by half step) from the 3rd–5th combination to the root–3rd combination over the V chord (D7) and the IV chord (C7), respectively.

A return to single-note playing at the start of the third chorus is a clever way to balance a longer solo. The spirit of the soulful bends in **bars 25–26** in a higher register begins to elevate the emotional level of the solo. Take a look at **bar 25**. You will also notice the use of the ♭5, which is a particularly bluesy tone. In fact, it is sometimes referred to as a blue note (along with ♭3 and ♭7).

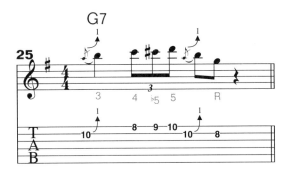

<table>
<tr><td>

Note on Enharmonic Respellings

Two notes that fall on the same fret (have the same pitch) but have different names are said to be *enharmonically equivalent*. For example, in **bar 25**, we see a C♯ instead of D♭ as the ♭5 of the G7 chord. *Respellings* such as this are used for ease of reading. They don't change the functions of the notes.

</td></tr>
</table>

A classic G Minor Pentatonic slide lick in **bar 27** continues to push the intensity of the solo as the notes move higher up the neck.

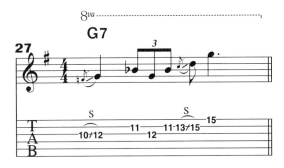

The use of *chromatic passing tones* (non-chord tones that connect two chord or scale tones by a half step) from within a triplet figure in **bar 29** continues to fuel the intensity of the solo in the higher register. The two passing tones on the 16th fret fit snugly between the chord tones of the IV chord (C7). Notice there is another example of enharmonic equivalents in this bar. The ♭3 is respelled as ♯2 for ease of reading.

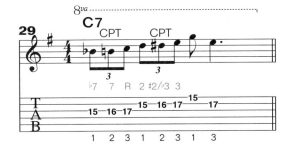

CPT = Chromatic passing tone

In **bar 32**, the solo is now structured firmly in the root position of the G Blues scale, but an octave higher starting at the 15th fret. Playing higher on the neck at the climax of the solo helps us reach a better emotional peak. The hammer-on from the ♭3rd (B♭) to the 3rd (B) resolves the line nicely against the I chord (G7).

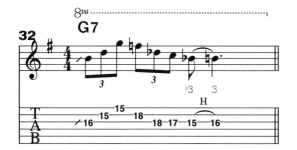

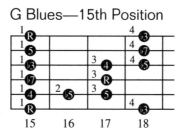

G Blues—15th Position

The bend at **bar 33** accentuates the F♯, the 3rd of the V chord (D7). The lick is a simple four-note *motif* that perfectly outlines the chord as the solo approaches the finish line. A motif is a short melodic or rhythmic figure that recurs throughout a piece of music.

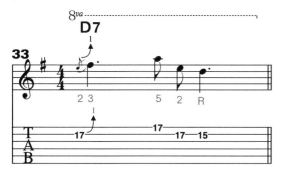

Observe that the motif from **bar 33** also appears in **bar 34**, now changed to fit the new chord. This is a cool device in shaping any solo. The listener hears a melodic continuity in the phrases as the notes ascend from the previous bar with a rousing bend into the 5th (G) against the IV chord (C7).

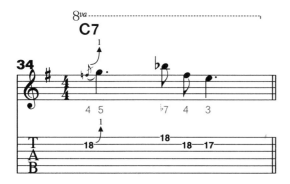

In Summary

When playing a longer solo, keep it simple at first and consider starting in a lower position and ascending the fretboard as intensity builds. Stress quality over the quantity of notes you play. Think about targeting chord tones and using expressive devices such as bends and slides.

DELTA BLUES

The term Delta blues refers to a style that originated in the Mississippi River Delta region. While Delta blues is largely an acoustic style, many of its characteristics are also used by electric players. Probably the greatest proponent of this style was Mississippi John Hurt.

This slow shuffle solo in the key of E covers two 12-bar choruses in a Delta blues style.

With Solo, Track 6
Backing Track, Track 7

Slow Delta Shuffle

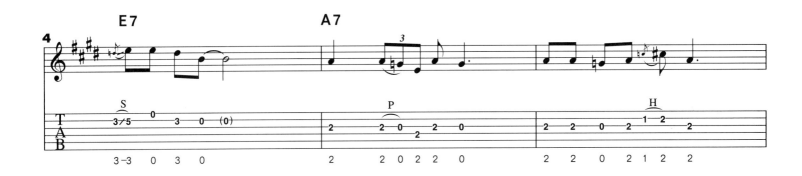

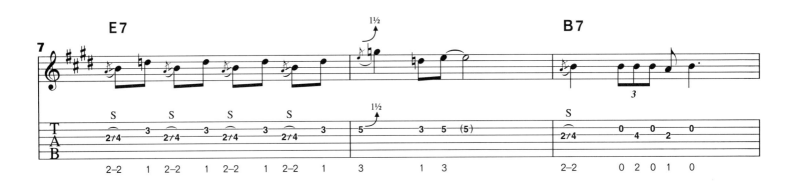

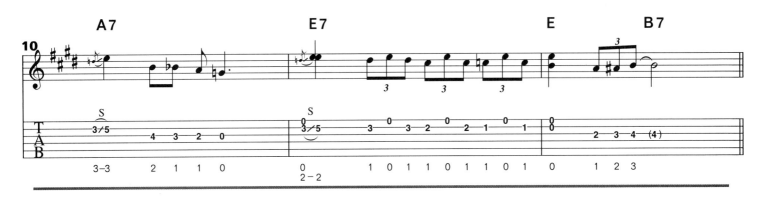

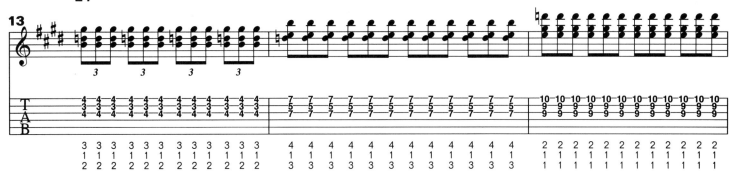

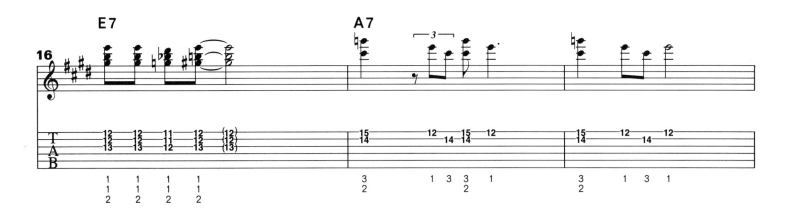

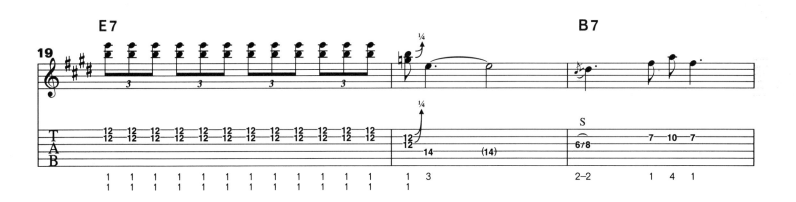

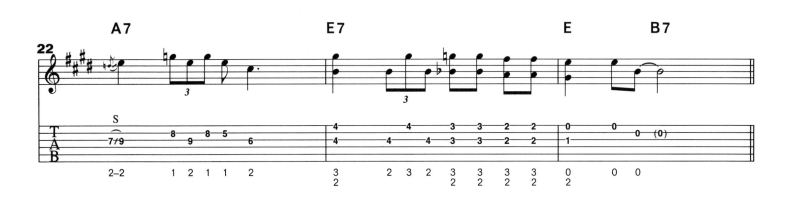

Analysis

The combination of lower and higher-note licks in **bars 1–4** creates a *call and response* theme, which is a great way to shape a Delta blues solo. In call and response phrasing, an initial *calling phrase* is followed by a response, which in some way answers the call. It is an almost conversational style of playing. Using as many slides, hammer-ons, and pull-offs as possible in the open position E Minor Pentatonic scale adds to the authenticity of this style.

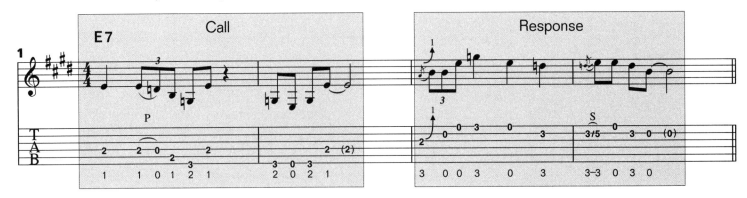

Since this solo is two choruses long, it starts off with some low register patterns from the E Minor Pentatonic scale that set the haunting Delta mood. **Bar 2** pauses on the root (E).

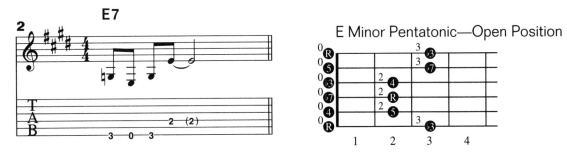

Notice that in **bar 4**, the notes of the E Minor Pentatonic scale shift to the top strings. Matching the open 1st string with a *unison slide* on the 2nd string is a classic Delta lick. In a unison slide, the unison (the same pitch) is struck simultaneously with the slide (a harmonic unison) on an adjacent string or directly afterward (a melodic unison).

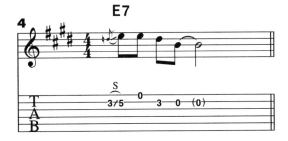

In **bar 5**, the spirit of the solo is kept alive by continuing to employ the E Minor Pentatonic scale, however the IV chord (A7) is highlighted by emphasizing its chord tones: root (A), ♭7th (G), and 5th (E).

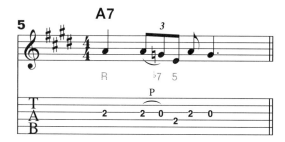

The repetitive slide lick in **bar 7** is a common way to drive the solo rhythmically and dramatically in the Delta blues style.

In **bar 9**, the classic unison lick returns. Notice the use of the ♭7th (A) with the root (B) over the V chord (B7).

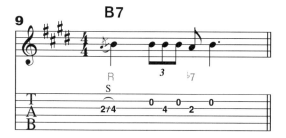

The beginning of the second chorus, **bars 13–15**, gets a fresh sound from moving through several three-note voicings of the I (E7) chord. This is a good contrast to the single-note texture of the first chorus.

In **bar 17**, the chord tones of the IV chord (A7) are plainly laid out. The double stops keep the Delta spirit alive. The double stops form a *tritone* consisting of the 3rd (C♯) and the ♭7th (G) over the A7 chord. (A tritone is an interval, the two notes of which are three whole steps away from each other.)

Bars 21–22 feature an arpeggio of each chord that fortifies the harmonies. The V and IV chords leading to the turnaround in **bars 23–24** are critical bars, calling for distinctive licks that tie the harmonic structure of the solo together.

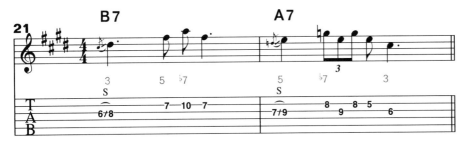

Summary

Some of the things you can do to create a Delta sound include using call and response phrasing, playings lots of slide licks, double-stops, three-note voicings, and executing slides and bends to notes followed by their unison pitches on adjacent strings.

ROCK BLUES

The hard edge and drive of rock music are blended with the blues in the rock-blues style. Perhaps the biggest proponent of the rock-blues style is Eric Clapton. This solo covers three choruses in a rock-blues style.

With Solo, Track 8
Backing Track, Track 9

Three That Rock

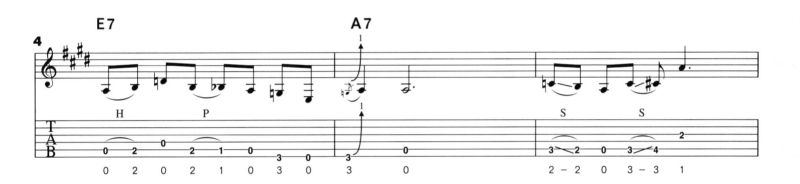

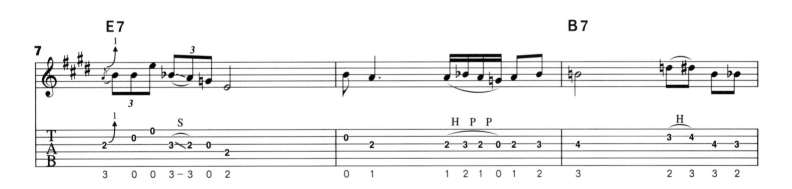

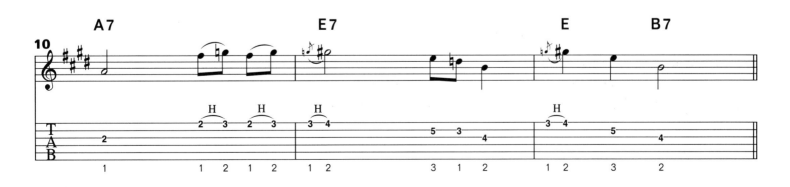

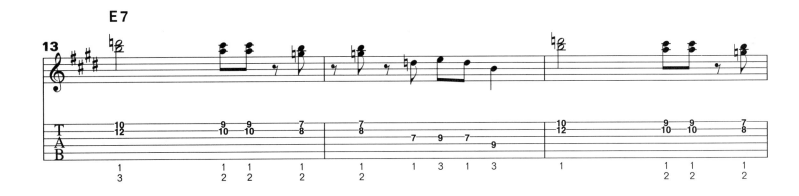

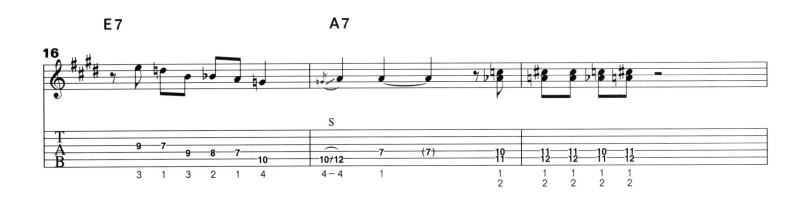

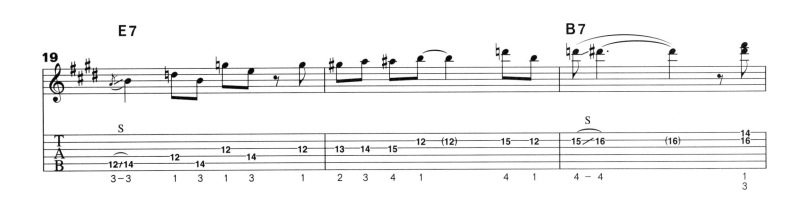

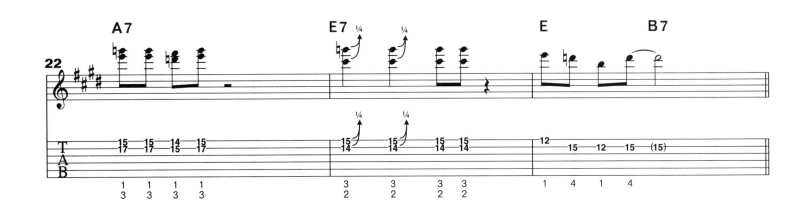

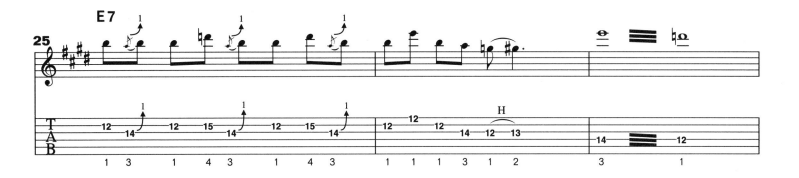

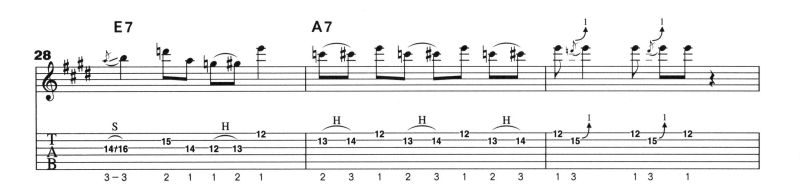

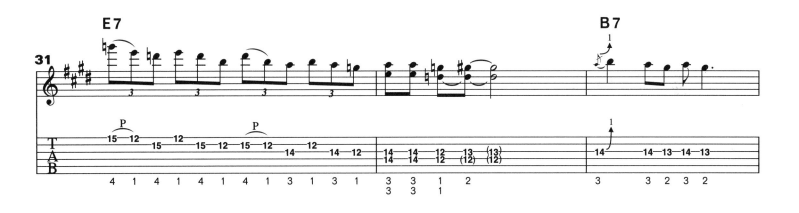

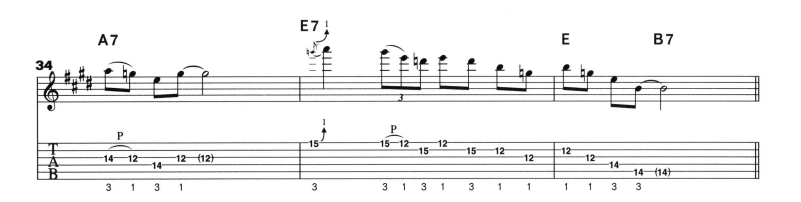

Analysis

The first chorus opens with open-position licks from the E Blues scale. A lot of these phrases are sped-up Delta blues licks. Once again, starting in open position and moving higher as the solo proceeds is a smart way to build a solo.

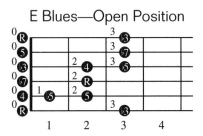

E Blues—Open Position

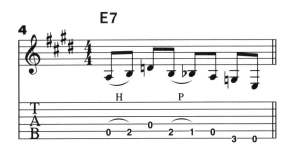

Sometimes, the simplest lick is the most effective. Check out **bar 5**. Here we have a bend from the ♭7th (G) up to the root (A) on the 6th string, followed by the unison on the open 5th string. You do not have to play a lot of notes to have a powerful lick; "less is more" is always a great blues strategy.

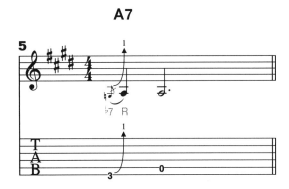

The rapid hammer-on and pull-off passage on beat three of **bar 8** energizes the solo with expression. This point of the chorus is always a great place to create a peak by playing a few quick notes with fretting-hand slurs.

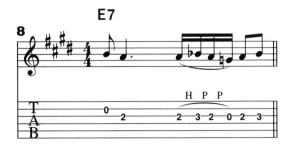

Bar 9 is an example of simplicity in lick construction. If you are playing lots and lots of notes, it's probably not very bluesy. Notice the hammer-on from the ♭3rd (D) to the 3rd (D♯) against the V chord (B7). This gives good support to the V chord.

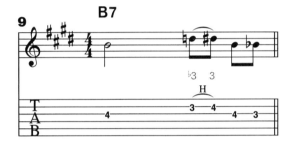

As you've seen in some of the turnarounds from the previous solos (page 17, bars 23–24 and page 25, bars 23–24), classic double-stop passages often neatly conclude a 12-bar chorus. In this style, try a concise, single-note theme that outlines the I chord (E7). Here it is—short and sweet.

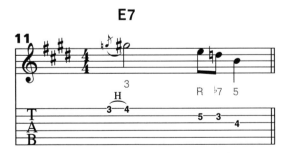

The second chorus opens at **bar 13** with a double-stop phrase in 3rds. This is a great way to thicken up a line.

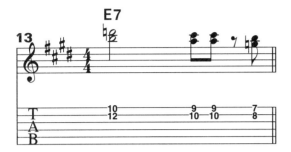

Notice the contrast of the two licks against the IV chord (A7) in **bars 17–18**: the stark sound of the two unison A notes in **bar 17** compared to the thicker sounds of the harmonic-3rd lick in **bar 18**. Also notice the sliding lick followed by the unison that was first introduced in **bar 5** as a bending/unison lick.

At **bar 19**, the solo picks up intensity with a driving rock-blues lick from the E Minor Pentatonic scale in 12th position. Continuing to use contrasting shapes and sounds is a good thing because it keeps the solo interesting.

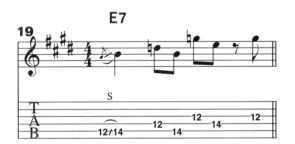

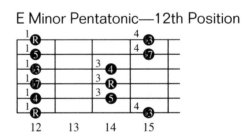

The slide into the 3rd (D#) of the V chord (B7) adds a touch of simplicity after the more complex sounds of the previous two bars. Since the V chord appears only near the end a 12-bar blues progression, playing a strong idea that reflects the harmony creates a tighter solo.

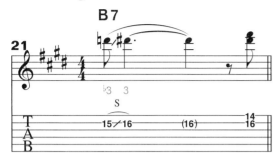

The double-stop idea reappears in **bar 22**, doing a nice job of balancing out the single-note lines. The double-stop 3rds emphasize the 5th (E) and the ♭7th (G) of the IV chord (A7).

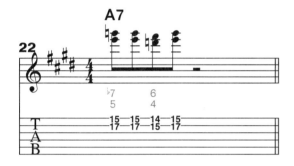

The chorus finishes with a rousing *quarter-tone*, double-stop bend on the turnaround. A quarter tone is an interval equal to one half of a half step. In this style, it is effective to end with a simple emotional cry.

At the beginning of the third chorus in **bar 25**, the solo gains intensity as it shifts to the upper register. Another way to build the intensity is to use a larger number of notes, as you can see happening in **bars 25–26**. Notice, however, that the licks remain simple and stay within the context of the E Minor Pentatonic scale. The bends keep things rocking in **bar 25**. **Bar 26** concludes with the resolution to the 3rd (G♯) of the I chord (E7).

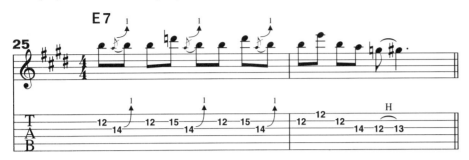

The simple, repetitive rhythmic figure in **bar 29** against the IV chord (A7) fuels the energy of this chorus.

The energy of the solo soars in **bar 31** with a triplet *sequence* (a motif repeated at different pitches) that descends through the E Minor Pentatonic scale in 12th position. This type of phrase is powerful in a rock-blues format.

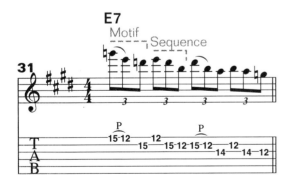

E Minor Pentatonic—12th Position

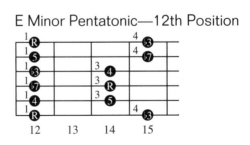

The structure of this chorus becomes thicker in **bar 32** as a classic double-stop idea in 4ths appears. The lick ends on a tritone made of the ♭7th (D) and the 3rd (G♯) of the I chord (E7).

One cool way to structure a V-chord lick is to use the Mixolydian mode on the corresponding root. In **bar 33**, three notes of the B Mixolydian mode are used over the V chord (B7). It starts with a bend from the ♭7th (A) to the root (B) and is followed by a back-and-forth motion between the ♭7th (A) and the 6th (G♯).

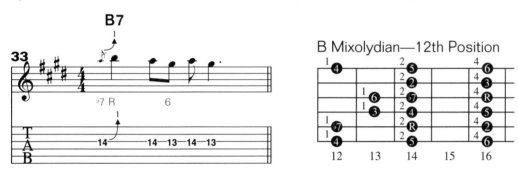

A strong bend followed by another sequenced pattern from the E Minor Pentatonic scale finishes the solo with a furious flurry of notes at the turnaround in **bar 35**.

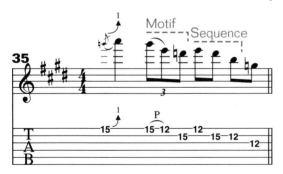

SLOW BLUES

Many players feel that slow blues is the most expressive of the blues styles. The slow tempo allows for a more emotional approach, plus it is easier to experiment with different harmonies and scales. This solo covers two 12-bar choruses in a slow-blues style.

With Solo, Track 10
Backing Track, Track 11

Two Slow

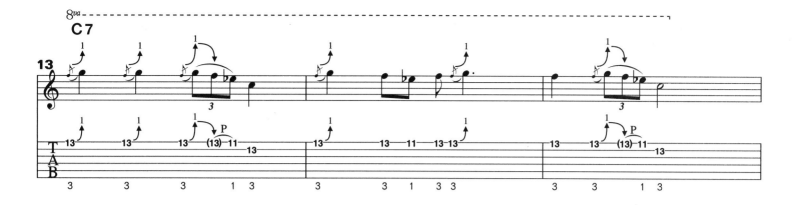

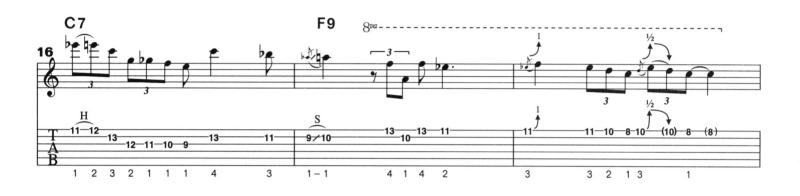

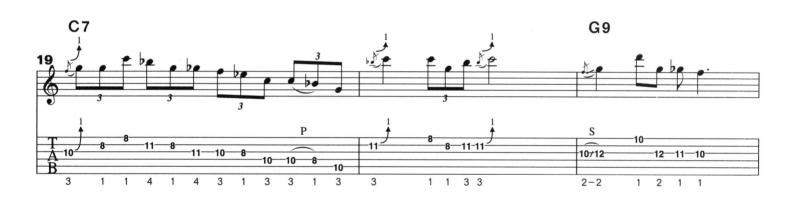

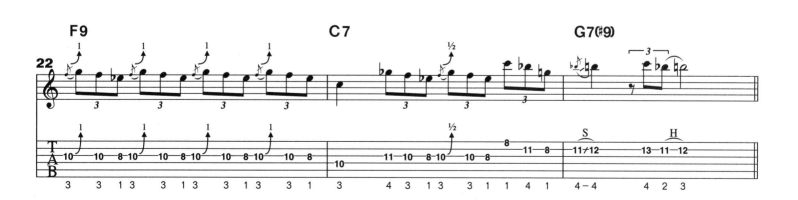

Analysis

Bars 1–4 set the tone by establishing a pattern of simple phrases with a lot of feeling. Primarily emphasizing chord tones creates a structure that is easy for the listener to understand.

Notice how **bars 1–4** stay in one area of the neck—mostly 5th position—and use soulful bends. The slide into the ♭7th (B♭) in **bar 4** brings out the dominant 7th flavor of the C7 chord. The dominant 7th is the quintessential blues chord: R–3–5–♭7. Getting the most out of notes in a single position helps create a unified structure for a slow blues solo.

A handy trick for playing over the IV chord is to use the corresponding composite major/minor pentatonic scale—in this case: F Major/Minor Composite. **Bar 6** exemplifies this. Because of the slower tempo, it is easier to change the scale for a specific chord.

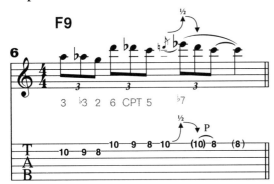

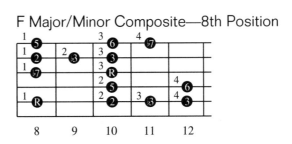

F Major/Minor Composite—8th Position

CPT = Chromatic Passing Tone

Bar 7 features a bluesy *bend, release, pull-off* combination. This technique imparts a colorful sound to a slow blues solo. Use it often.

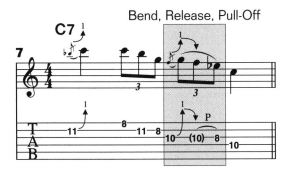

Bar 9 features a slick chromatic run over the V chord (G9). The lick starts with a bend into the 3rd (B), then makes its way chromatically to the 5th (D). The lick ends with another bend into the B and a return to the root (G). The V chord is the harmonic climax of the 12-bar form, so the lick you play over it is crucial.

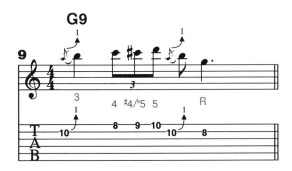

Bar 10 highlights a repetitive triplet figure on the root (F) against the IV chord (F9). Sometimes a simple rhythmic idea works more effectively than a complex run. You also want to pace yourself; if you throw in a complex barrage of notes too early, you are going to be hard pressed to come up with a stronger statement in the second chorus.

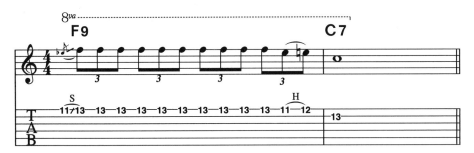

The intensity of the second chorus rises at **bar 13**, setting the tone with consecutive bends. The solo shifts into the upper register, which also raises the energy level. The licks are still simple and come from the C Minor Pentatonic scale.

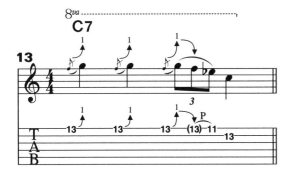

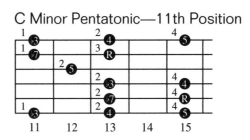

C Minor Pentatonic—11th Position

A strong triplet figure featuring the chord tones of the I chord (C7) in **bar 16** is a smooth way to contrast the bending licks of the previous three bars.

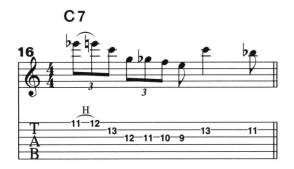

Using a dominant 7th chord-tone lick is a cool way to play over the IV chord (F9). At a change to a new chord, playing a phrase that clearly states the notes of the new chord helps define its harmony and is great material for a musical lick.

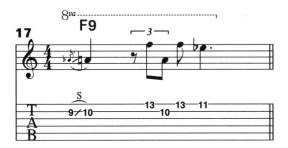

With the return of the I chord (C7) in **bar 19**, the solo returns to a hard-driving C Blues lick that is effective here because of the consecutive triplets. The rhythm of a phrase either maintains or changes the amount of activity, so it is just as important as the harmonic content in shaping a solo. For example, a bar with two half notes or four quarter notes would not be as active as a bar filled with eight-note triplets, and would therefore have a much different effect on the solo.

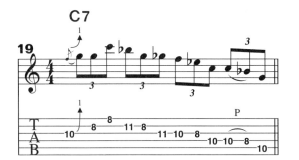

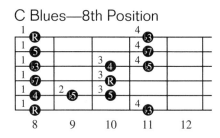

In **bar 21**, the tones of the V chord (G9) are accented in a string-skipping lick. It outlines the root (G), the 5th (D), and the ♭7th (F). Keep the simplicity of the phrase in mind here—make a strong statement over the V chord.

The repeated three-note motif in **bar 22** drives the solo to a strong conclusion.

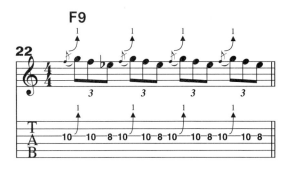

This is a slow blues solo that spans three 12-bar choruses in the key of A.

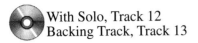With Solo, Track 12
Backing Track, Track 13

Blue Three Times

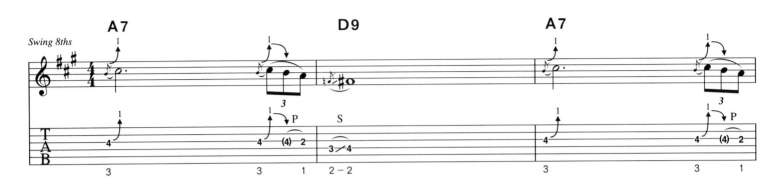

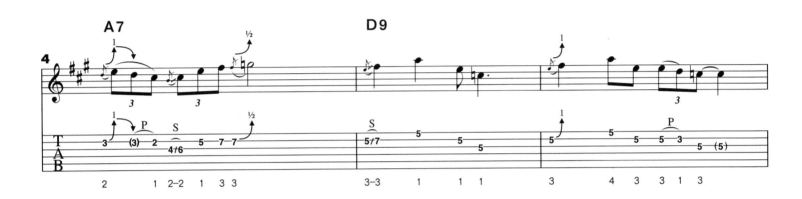

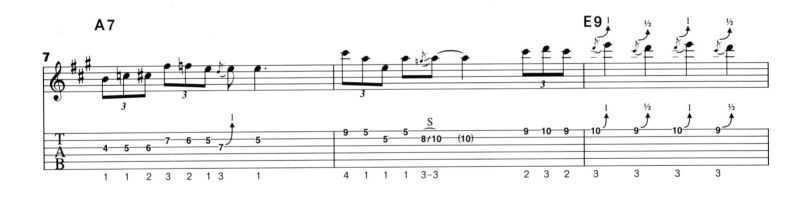

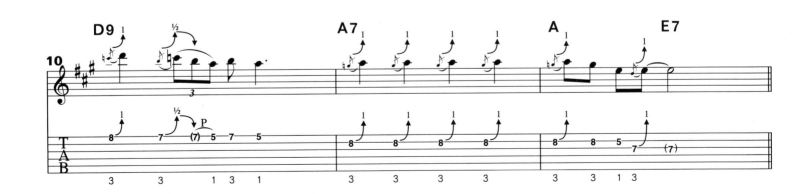

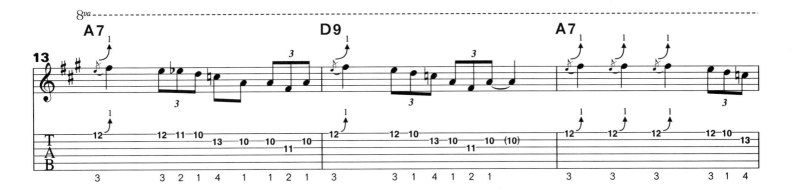

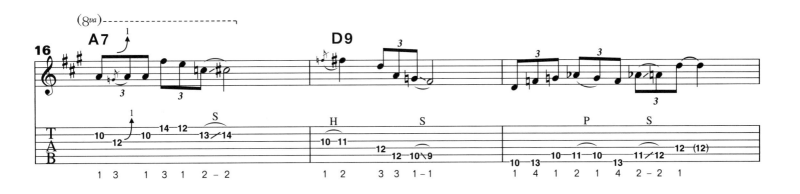

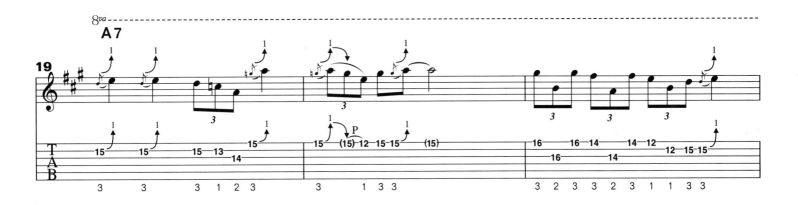

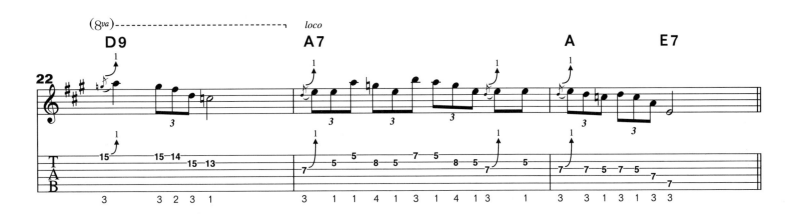

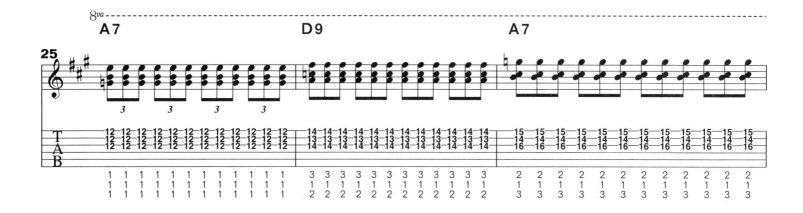

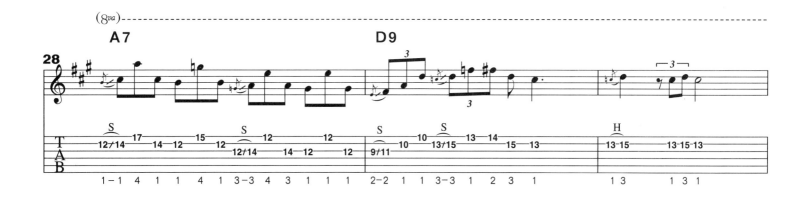

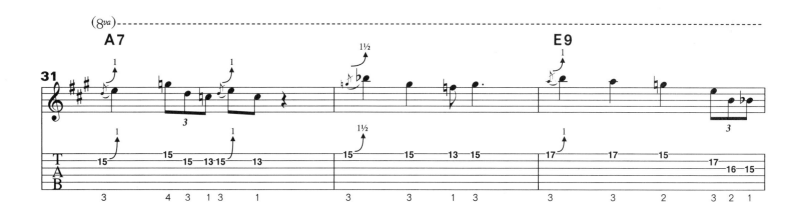

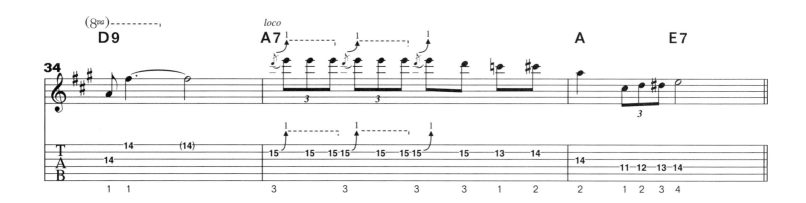

Analysis

In this longer slow blues solo, the "quality over quantity" approach to note selection is taken. A set of bending licks is a strong way to open the first chorus in **bar 1**. The major pentatonic scale lends a sense of simplicity to the beginning of a multi-chorus solo because it does not contain any altered or blue notes ($\flat 3$, $\flat 5$, or $\flat 7$). The root (A), 3rd (C$\sharp$), and 9th (B) from the A Major Pentatonic scale create a more understated ambience. **Bar 2** features a slide into the 3rd (F$\sharp$) of the *quick change* IV chord (D9). Quick change, sometimes called *quick four*, refers to the use of the IV chord in the second bar of a 12-bar blues.

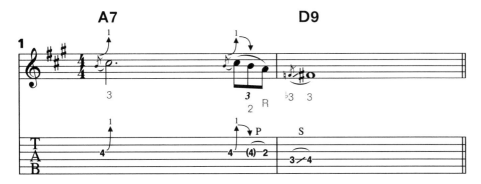

A Major Pentatonic—2nd Position

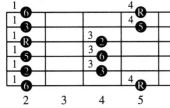

Targeting the chord tones of the IV chord (D9) in **bar 5** is essential because a listener can more easily lose track of the harmonic structure at this slower tempo.

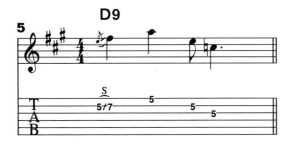

Bar 7 continues to employ the A Major Pentatonic scale, but notice in **bar 8** the presence of the A Minor Pentatonic scale due to the C♮ falling squarely on the *downbeat* (first beat in the bar). Combining these two scales is a great way to build a solo. Remember, the minor pentatonic includes two blue notes: ♭3 and ♭7. The use of these blue notes starts to push the solo into a bluesier realm.

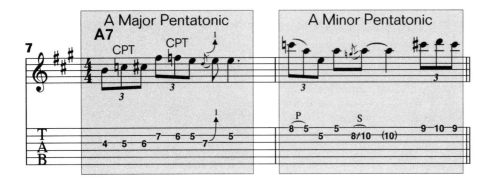

CPT = Chromatic passing tone

A Major Pentatonic—4th Position

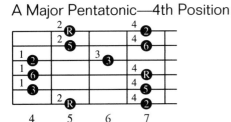

A Minor Pentatonic—5th Position

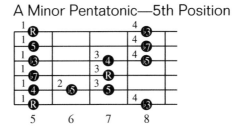

Remember that **bar 9**—the first place the V chord appears—is the critical turning point of the 12-bar blues progression. The simple, repetitive quarter-note bends that highlight the ♭7 (D) and the root (E) are a relief after the busy quality of the previous bars.

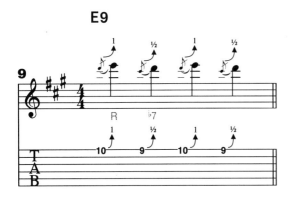

Bar 10 follows the harmony with a simple D Mixolydian phrase that includes the root (D), ♭7th (C), 6th (B), and the 5th (A).

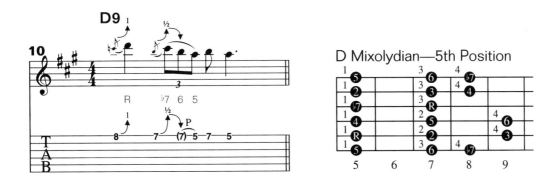

As the second chorus begins in **bar 13**, we move up to the 12th fret. The similarities between **bars 13–14** creates a unified idea as the chords change; the lick is played over the I chord (A7) and again with slight variation over the IV chord (D9).

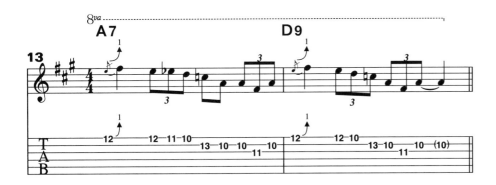

As the IV chord (D9) appears in **bar 17**, notice the use of a D7 arpeggio that nicely outlines the chord. The G on the 10th fret of the 5th string is the 4th of the chord. It is a slick tone to place in between the 5th and 3rd of the arpeggio that creates a musically satisfying lick.

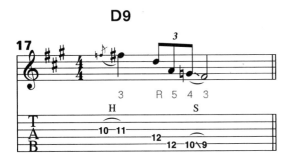

The strong bending lick in **bar 19** heightens the intensity of the solo. The A Minor Pentatonic scale—particularly the ♭3rd (C)—gives the solo a bluesy edge against the I chord (A7), which has a non-altered 3rd (C♯). Notice the octave string skip on the last beat of the bar: This is a powerful tool that adds energy.

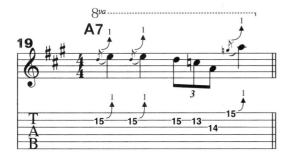
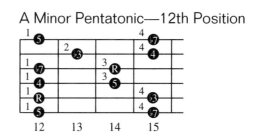

A Minor Pentatonic—12th Position

Another cool string skipping technique appears in **bar 21** over the V chord (E9). The two triplets are melodic 6th intervals that help the overall balance between adjacent and non-adjacent string patterns in the solo.

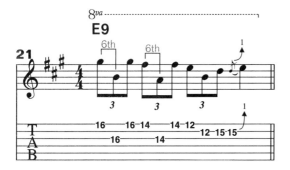

The turnaround of the second chorus, **bars 23–24**, should drive hard toward the opening of the third chorus. The consecutive triplets lend rhythmic intensity while the solo rocks out with the A Minor Pentatonic scale. The 9th (B) adds a colorful tinge to the bluesier pentatonic scale tones.

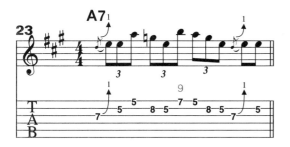

The first three bars of the last chorus (**bars 25–27**) open with triads driven by repetitive triplet eighth-note figures. The triads add harmonic depth to the solo by outlining and/or coloring the underlying chords while the triplets fuel the solo rhythmically.

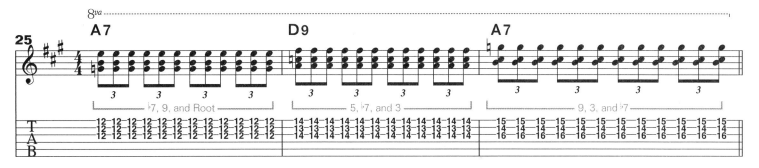

The use of the triplet figure continues in **bar 28**. Using more notes and less space is okay at this point in the solo as it energizes the final chorus. The adjacent-string 6th interval motif (with one 5th) adds a nice melodic contour to the line. All the notes in this bar come from the A Mixolydian mode, a colorful contrast to the heavy use of pentatonic scales common in blues improvisation.

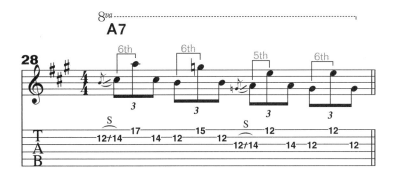

A Mixolydian—12th Position

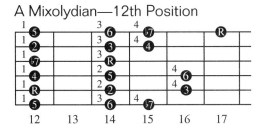

In **bar 29**, the solo remains rhythmically busy. This keeps the energy at a high level. The ♭3rd (F) adds a bluesy touch to the D7 arpeggio lick over the IV chord (D9).

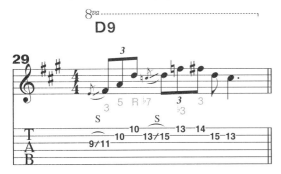

Bar 32 features a minor 3rd bend (the distance in pitch of three half steps) from the ♭7 (G) to the ♭9 (B♭) over the I chord (A7). As the solo peaks, a wailing effect of a wide bend catches the audience's attention because it is so different from the more predictable half- and whole-step bends. Also, the ♭9 is a very colorful tone.

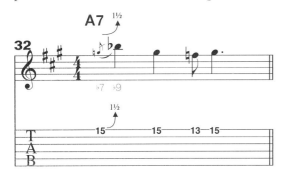

At **bar 33**, the solo moves to the highest fret of the chorus with a whole-step bend on the 17th fret. A lick that strongly emphasizes the chord tones (root, 3rd, 5th) over the V chord supports the solo harmonically and leads to a solid conclusion.

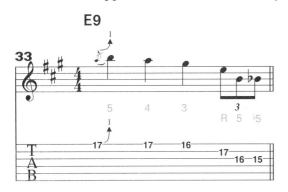

Summary

For a sweet slow blues solo, use lots of bends, simple motifs, and repetitive rhythmic themes. Stress quality over quantity and target the blue notes. Use devices such as chromatic passing tones and intervallic string-skipping licks to vary the melodic contour. Also, remember that wide bends of one-and-a-half steps will create emotional wailing sounds that are perfect for a slow blues.

BLUES IN THE STYLE OF "STORMY MONDAY"

"They Call It Stormy Monday (But Tuesday Is Just as Bad)," by Aaron "T-Bone" Walker, is one of the most-played, most-imitated blues tunes ever written. It has been covered by everybody from Big Joe Turner (in the 1950s) to the Allman Brothers Band (in the 1970s). This solo covers one chorus of a slow blues in the style of "Stormy Monday."

With Solo, Track 14
Backing Track, Track 15

Stormy

Analysis

The first half of this solo, **bars 1–6**, uses the G Minor Pentatonic scale.

G Minor Pentatonic—3rd Position

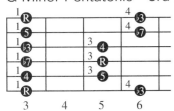

Bar 2 has the quick change to the IV chord (C). Because of the slower tempo, it is a good idea to switch to the C Major Pentatonic scale in this bar. The C Major Pentatonic scale accents the root (C), the 3rd (E), the 5th (G), and the 6th (A). In a blending of scales that is typical of the blues, the ♭7 from the C Minor Pentatonic scale also appears.

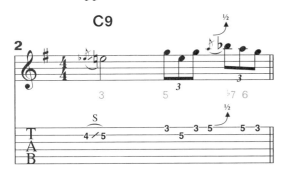

C Major Pentatonic—2nd Position

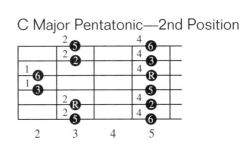

The bending phrase in **bar 3** brings back the tonality of the G Minor Pentatonic scale over the I chord (G). The bend, release, pull-off combination (introduced on page 41) is a very colorful, effective sound for this part of the solo.

The driving triplet figures in **bar 4** moving down the G Blues scale increase the intensity of the solo as it moves toward the IV chord in **bar 5**.

G Blues—5th Position

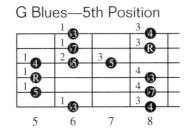

The soulful bends to the 3rd (E) in **bar 5** support and help define the IV chord (C9).

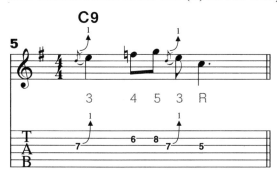

At **bar 7**, the harmonic structure of the solo becomes more complex. The chord progression begins to walk part of the way up the harmonized *chord scale* (every note in a scale harmonized with triads or 7th chords) of G Major: GMaj7, Amin7, Bmin7, B♭min7 (*passing chord,* or chord outside the key, placed between two diatonic chords) to the Amin7 in **bar 9**. Therefore, use the G Major Pentatonic scale to accommodate the new tonality. Also, notice the use of the bend, release, pull-off combination on beat 2.

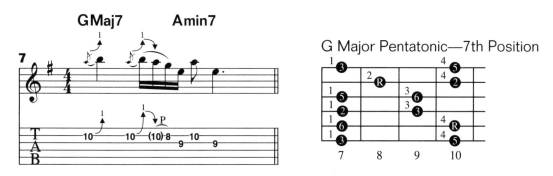

Here is the G Major chord scale:

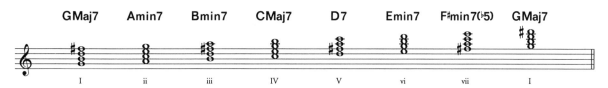

As mentioned above, the B♭min7 chord in **bar 8** is a passing chord between the iii chord (Bmin7) and the ii chord (Amin7). Notice the A♭, the ♭7th of the B♭min7, played against this chord.

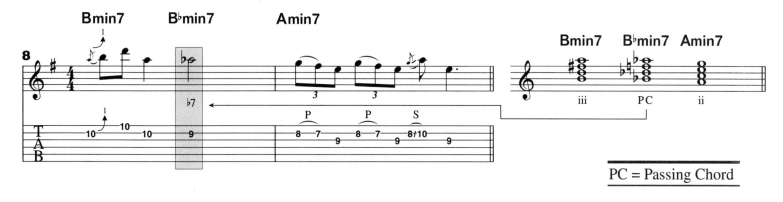

PC = Passing Chord

In **bar 9**, the intensity of the solo is rhythmically charged by the use of a repetitive triplet figure. The pull-off and slide techniques add extra punch to the line. The melodic material still comes from the G Major Pentatonic scale.

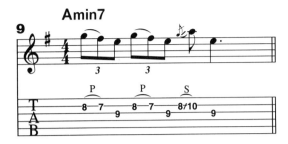

The A♭Maj7 chord in **bar 10** is a chromatic passing chord that makes for a smooth move from the Amin7 to the G7 as the solo moves toward the turnaround. A simple minor-3rd bend highlighting the 3rd (C) and the 5th (E♭) maintains the integrity of the blues sound over this *outside* (not in the key) chord.

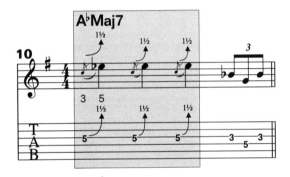

Summary

Changing scales as the chords change works well for a solo over changes in the style of "Stormy Monday." As the chord progression becomes more jazzy, walking up the chord scale, stick to the G Major Pentatonic scale and tried-and-true blues devices, such as bends, to maintain the integrity of the blues sound.

MINOR BLUES

If there's any style more bluesy than slow blues, it's minor blues. In minor blues, the 12-bar form is essentially the same, but the chords are minor, making the sound even more "blue." This solo covers one 12-bar chorus in a minor-blues style. Notice how this solo uses straight 8ths instead of the more common swing 8ths.

With Solo, Track 16
Backing Track, Track 17

Minor Blues in A

Analysis

A hard-driving A Minor arpeggio opens the solo with conviction in **bar 2** after a whole note in **bar 1**. The repetition of chord tones establishes the minor sound right from the start.

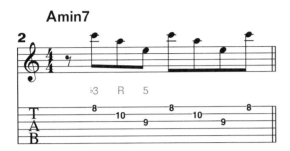

The two-note *string sweep* from the A Minor Pentatonic scale in **bar 4** gives the solo a strong, biting feel. Execute this technique by using one upstroke across two adjacent strings—in this case from the 1st to the 2nd strings. Make sure you make contact with both strings in one, fluid right-hand motion. These short sweeps add a lot of expression to a blues solo. The A Minor Pentatonic scale is very effective in an A Minor blues solo because the notes of the scale mimic the notes of the Amin7 chord: root (A), ♭3rd (C), 5th (E), and ♭7th (G).

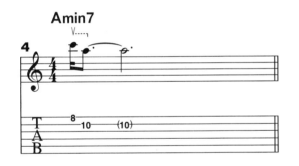

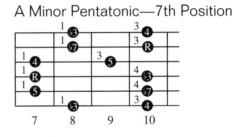

In **bar 6**, the minor-3rd bend is a powerful sound against the iv chord (Dmin7). The root (D) bends to the ♭3rd (F) creating a colorful chord-tone sound.

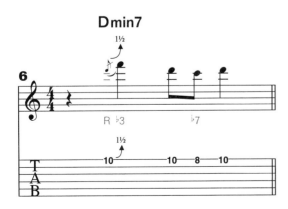

Bar 8 mimics the rhythm in **bar 2** and uses a higher inversion of the A Minor arpeggio. Repeating a previous lick with slight variations—such as the inversion of an arpeggio—gives listeners something they can identify, a hook. It helps make the solo easier to follow.

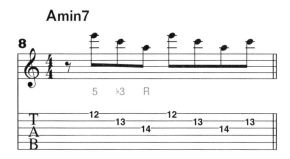

In **bar 9**, the F chord comes along. It is the VI chord in the key of A Minor. Playing a lick out of the A Natural Minor scale (Aeolian mode) is a nice melodic choice for this harmony. The opening bend sounds the major 7th (E), a sweet note to add to the F chord.

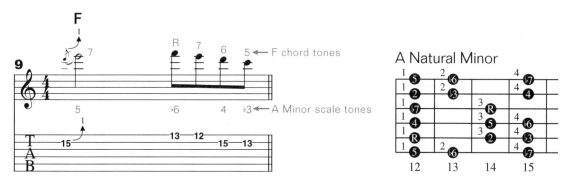

An Emin7 arpeggio is used over the v chord (Emin7) in **bar 10**. Using the corresponding arpeggio over each minor 7th chord is a strong way to structure licks in a minor blues solo.

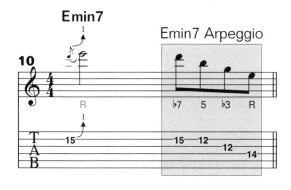

This solo covers one 12-bar chorus in a minor blues style. Like the previous solo, this one uses straight 8ths.

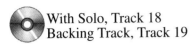

With Solo, Track 18
Backing Track, Track 19

Eighths Straight, No Chaser

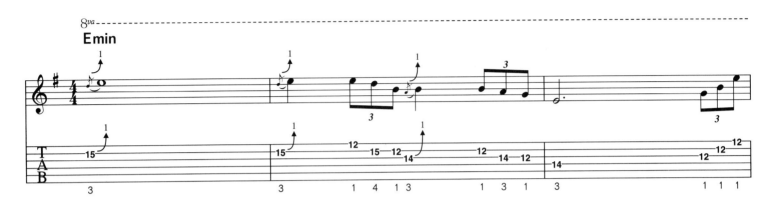

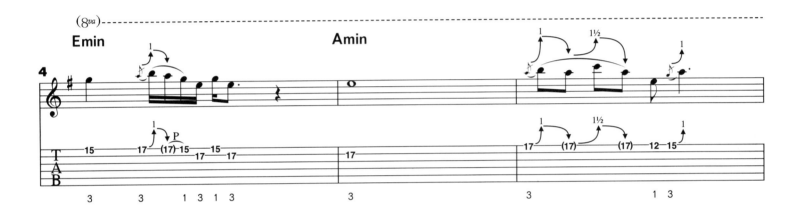

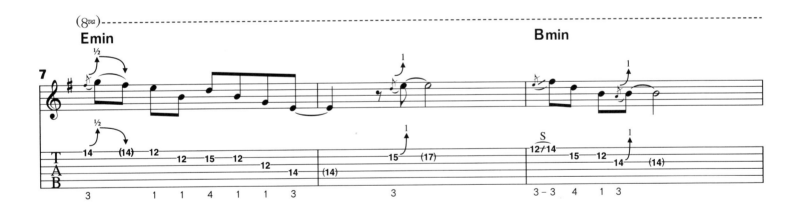

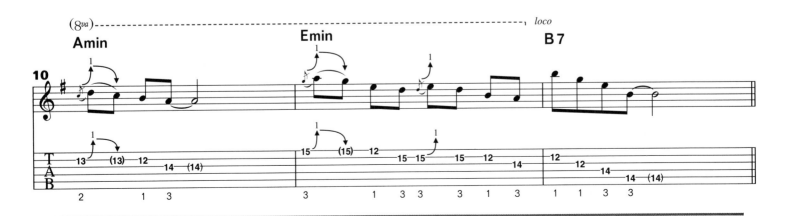

Analysis

A cool method for opening a solo is to bend into a note and hold it throughout
bar 1. Give it some vibrato, and you're off to an attention-grabbing start.

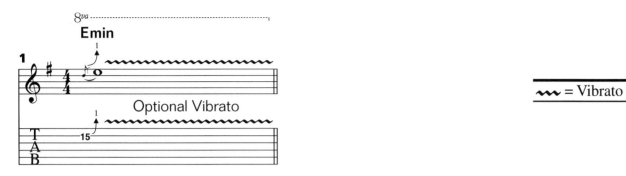

$\sim\!\sim$ = Vibrato

The E Minor arpeggio phrase in **bar 3** returns the solo to a simplistic mood after a
flurry of notes from the E Minor Pentatonic scale in **bar 2**.

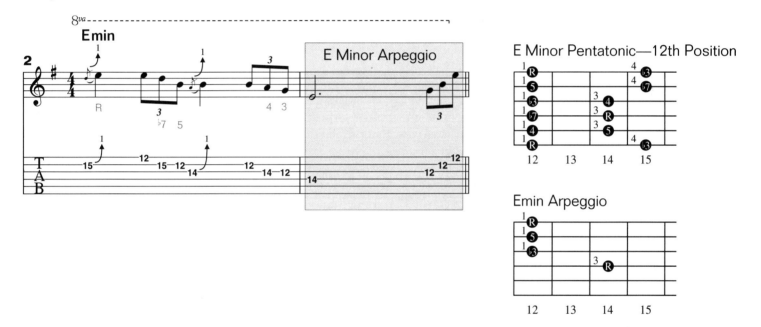

Creating a contrast between consecutive bars makes for sweet phrasing. In **bar 5**,
silence is golden; in **bar 6** the wailing consecutive bends provide a great difference.
In the consecutive bends, there is a bend and release followed by a wider bend and
release. This is all done on one pick stroke.

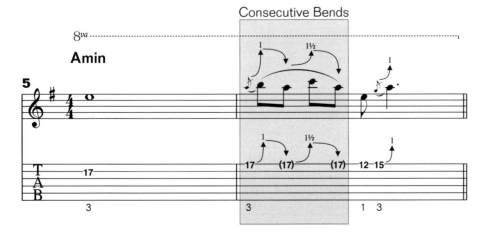

The intensity picks up in **bar 7**. The opening half-step bend and release features the 9th (F♯). This is a colorful tone to "lean" on while shaping a minor blues solo, as it lends a nice contrast to the minor pentatonic phrases.

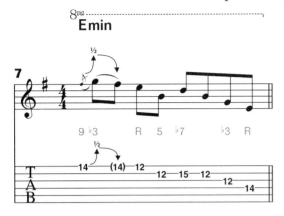

The B Minor arpeggio is a solid choice for improvising over the v chord (Bmin), because all of the chord tones are in the E Natural Minor scale. As we have seen, emphasizing the chord tones helps clarify the harmonies in the solo.

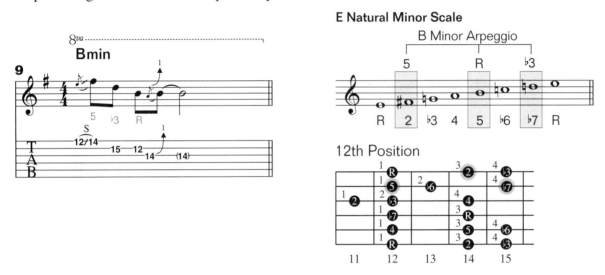

The notes in **bar 10** are pulled from the A Natural Minor scale, which offers a nice contrast to the arpeggio and pentatonic licks in the previous bars. The bend and release keeps the solo bluesy even though the notes come from the minor scale, which is not typically thought of as having a blues sound. Use bends as often as you can for more expression.

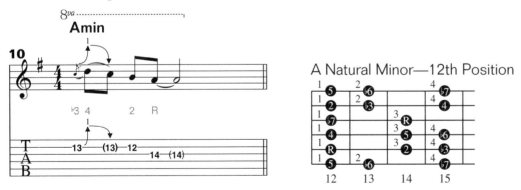

Summary

The minor blues uses a similar 12-bar form as the previous examples but with minor chords and straight 8ths. Use lots of vibrato and contrast to be expressive. The Aeolian mode (natural minor scale) in the key of the i chord will work for all of the chords, as will the minor pentatonic scale, which has all its notes in common with the Aeolian mode. As always, arpeggios are good sources for note choices over any chord.

FUNK BLUES

Funk blues is fueled by punchy eighth-note grooves and features blues licks set against funk rhythms rather than the traditional shuffle and rock rhythms. This style began in the early 1960s Chicago-blues era with guitarists Magic Sam and Buddy Guy. Classic funk blues tunes include "Watermelon Man" by Herbie Hancock, "Cissy's Strut" by The Meters, "I Just Want a Little Bit" by Magic Sam, and "Just Playing My Axe" by Buddy Guy. This solo covers one 12-bar chorus in a funk-blues style which calls for straight 8ths.

With Solo, Track 20
Backing Track, Track 21

In a Blues Funk

Analysis

The use of chromatic runs and double-stop patterns highlights **bars 1–3** of this chorus. In this style, you can get away with more activity in the solo. The lick beginning in **bar 1** resolves fluidly in **bar 2** with a hammer-on to the 3rd (E) and the root (C) over the I chord (C7). You can structure any of the 12 notes we have to work with any way you wish; just try to land on a chord tone at the end of a phrase. The double-stop lick in **bar 3** adds depth to the solo and is common in this style.

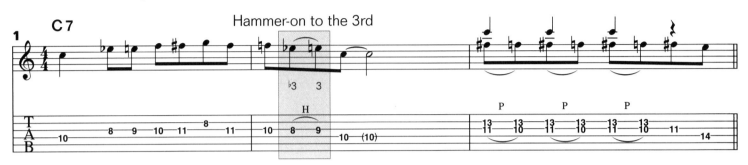

A short, repeating melodic lick in **bar 5** establishes a tight, funky musical groove. The lick is played over the IV chord (F7) and comes from the C Minor Pentatonic scale, a nice contrast to the more active licks in the previous bars.

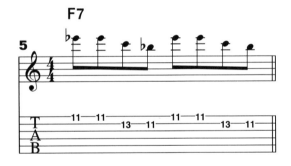

C Minor Pentatonic—11th Position

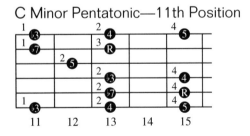

Bars 7–8 feature a colorful descending interval lick (major 7th, octave, minor 6th) that is often used by keyboard players. Taking ideas from other instruments and transferring them to the guitar fretboard is a creative way to formulate new ideas. Notice the leaping motion with wide intervals on non-adjacent strings. This is a great way to balance the use of stepwise motion in the rest of your solo.

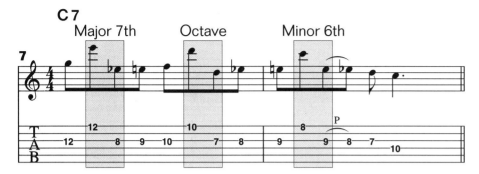

Once again, a short melodic figure in **bar 9** keeps the solo in a concise and musical groove. Playing licks like this keeps you from overplaying and losing the interest of the listener. This is played over the V chord (G7), a great place for this type of lick.

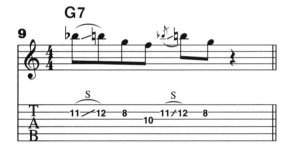

A strong chord-tone lick in **bar 10** over the IV chord (F7) drives the solo home. The half-step slide into the 3rd of the F7 (A) sets up this expressive lick. Using slides, hammer-ons, and pull-offs often captures the essence of this style.

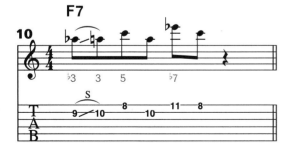

Summary
Expect straight 8ths in the funk-blues style. Play very rhythmically, focusing on short melodic phrases using plenty of slides, hammer-ons, and pull-offs.

JUMP BLUES

Jump blues refers to an uptempo, jazz-tinged style of blues that first came to prominence in the mid to late 1940s. Usually featuring a vocalist in front of a large, horn-driven orchestra or medium-sized combo with multiple horns, the style is distinguished by a driving rhythm, intensely shouted vocals, and honking tenor saxophone solos—a precursor to rock 'n' roll. This solo covers one 12-bar chorus in a medium swing, jump-blues style.

With Solo, Track 22
Backing Track, Track 23

Jump!

Analysis

The rhythmic drive is the primary force of a jump-blues solo. **Bar 1** starts with a quick double-stop eighth-note tritone shout followed by rests and finishes with a similar eighth-note figure. Double stops are characteristic of this style.

After a bar of inactivity, **bar 3** erupts with a classic hot lick from the G Blues scale with an added 9 (2) in a pull-off triplet phrase, generating another rhythmic theme. The multitude of notes played in this bar stands in stark contrast to the previous two bars.

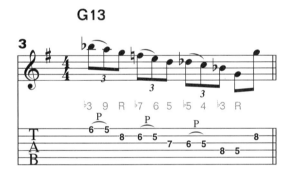

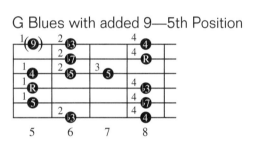

The chromatic walk into a rootless G13 voicing in **bar 4** puts the finishing touches on a well-balanced series of ideas over the I chord (G13).

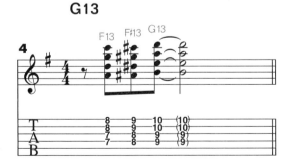

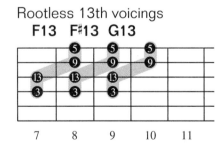

Chordal playing continues in **bars 5–6**. Notice the major-6th voicing over the C9 chord in **bar 5**: This voicing is used a lot in jump blues. Also notice the half-step movement from below into each chord.

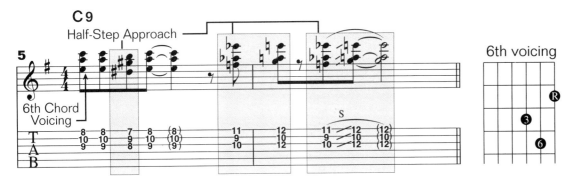

The sequenced triplet figure in **bar 7** recalls the rhythmic pattern from **bar 3**. This motivic approach helps to maintain a unified sense of phrasing throughout the chorus. The chromatic run (a mostly stepwise lick characterized by half steps) is a great way to add color and energy to the solo over the I chord (G13). At **bar 8**, the phrase resolves smoothly to the 3rd (B) followed by the root (G). The triad figure at the end of **bar 8** brings back the short eighth-note stabs from **bar 1**.

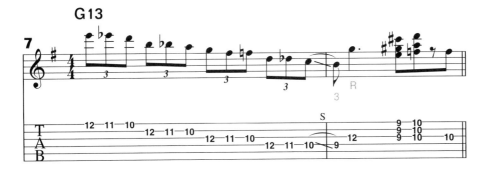

The lick played in **bar 9** is sequenced in **bar 10** using the same rhythm with the notes transposed down a whole step. This is an effective way to shape a solo, particularly over the V and IV chords in **bars 9** and **10**. Each bar uses each chord's corresponding major pentatonic scale (D, then C).

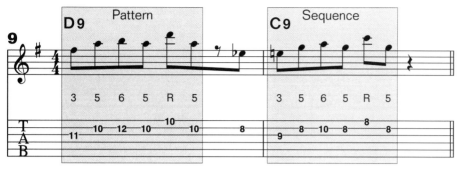

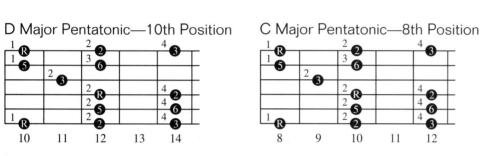

The turnaround beginning in **bar 11** is a classic descending run from the root (G) to the 5th (D) over the I chord (G7). The double-stop lick in **bar 12** caps off the balanced blend of single-note and double-stop licks used throughout the solo. The major 3rd intervals walk up chromatically from the IV to the V chord to wrap up the solo.

This solo covers two 12-bar choruses in a medium-fast swing jump-blues style.

With Solo, Track 24
Backing Track, Track 25

Swing, Jump 'n' Roll

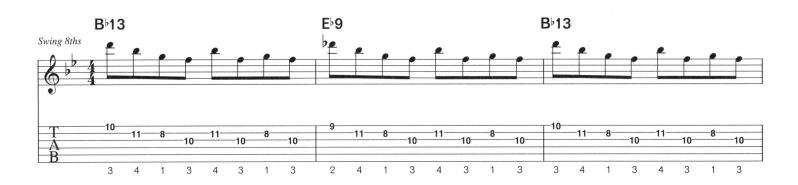

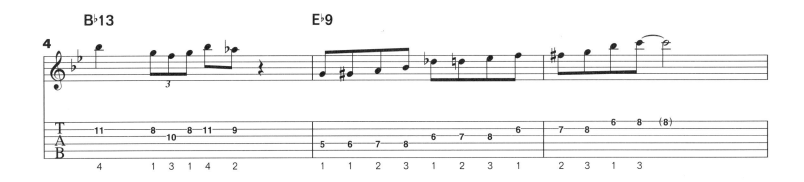

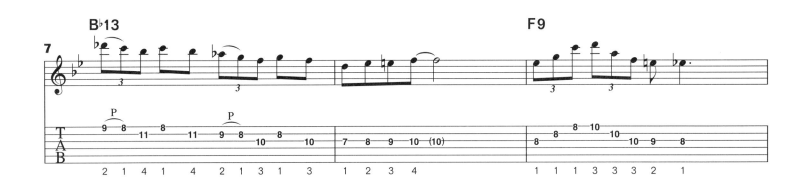

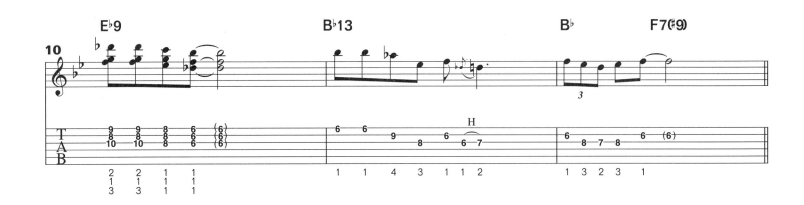

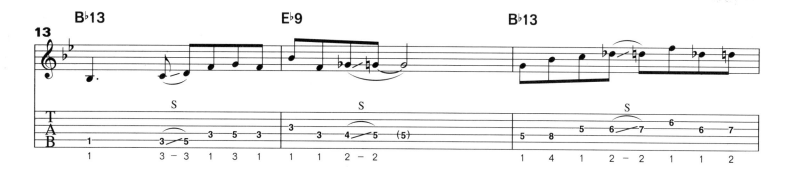

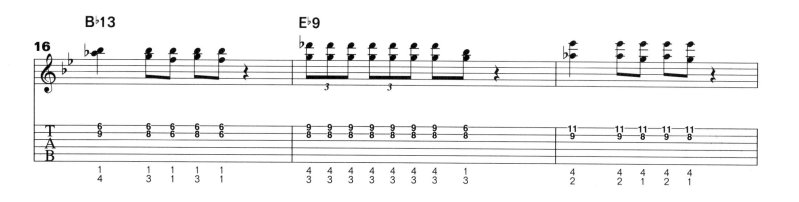

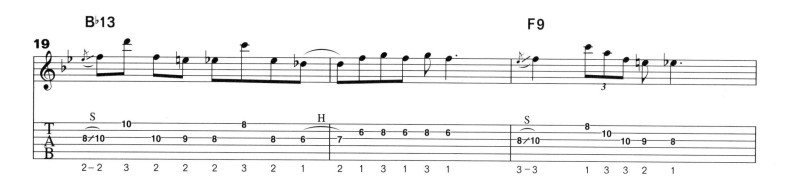

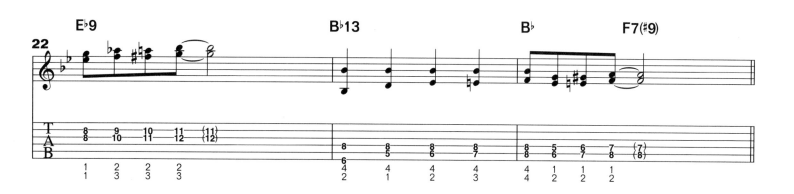

Analysis

Using a repeated motif in the opening two bars is a slick way to generate a solid, musical solo. The lick in **bar 2** is exactly the same as the lick in **bar 1** with the exception of the first note. This lick, built mostly from the B♭ Major Pentatonic scale, starts in **bar 1** with the 3rd (D) of the IV chord (E♭) but in **bar 2** starts with the ♭7 (D♭) of the E♭9 chord.

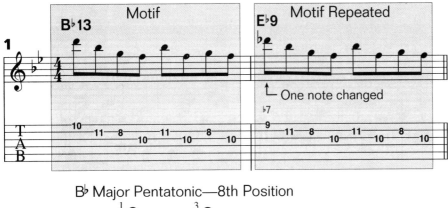

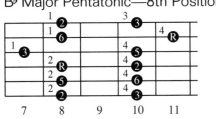

The chromatic run over the IV chord (E♭9) in **bar 5** keeps the intensity of the solo at a high level. Notice the consistent use of consecutive eighth notes, which maintains a solid rhythmic theme. The lick commences on the 3rd (G) of the E♭9 chord and ends on the 13th (C) in **bar 6**.

A good example of a sequenced rhythmic/melodic motif appears in **bar 7** over the I chord (B♭13). This hot B♭ Mixolydian figure descends with a finger-friendly pull-off combination that is punctuated by two consecutive triplet/eighth-note figures. Rhythmic themes such as these create a smooth sound that keeps the solo cooking.

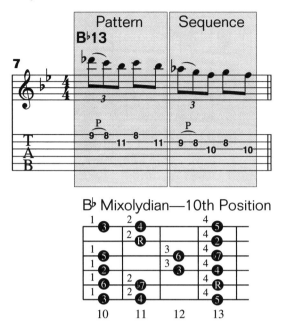

The eighth-note triplet arpeggio lick that ascends on the 8th fret and descends on the 10th fret in **bar 9**, followed by the chromatic resolution to the ♭7th (E♭) over the V chord (F9), provides a nice contrast to the stepwise licks in previous bars.

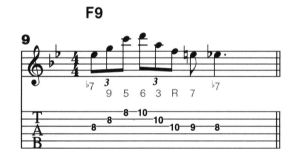

In this style, it is good to contrast the single-note lines with harmonic licks that reflect the chord changes. The lick in **bar 10** against the IV chord (E♭9) moves from a higher inversion of the chord to a lower inversion on the 6th fret.

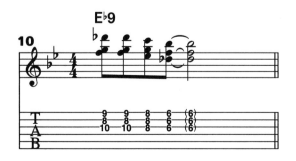

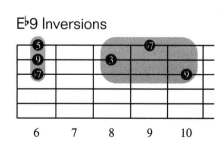

A drop to the lower register occurs in **bar 13** with the beginning of the second chorus. This can be an effective tool for structuring a balanced solo. The simplicity of the line, built from the B♭ Major Pentatonic scale, is a subtle way to begin this chorus.

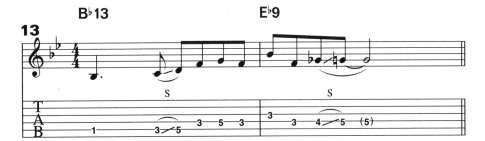

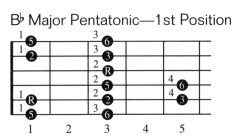

Bar 16 serves as a contrast to the previous bars with a double-stop phrase that moves through the B♭ Mixolydian scale. This thickens the sound of the notes used over the I chord (B♭13).

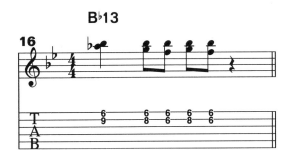

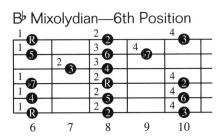

The tonal density, the thickness of tone created by the double stops, remains intact as the chords move from I in **bar 16** to IV in **bar 17**. The double-stop lick continues in **bar 17** over the IV chord (E♭9), accenting the tones of the chord.

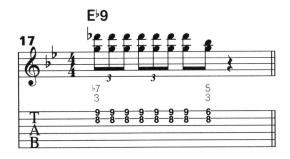

As the solo returns to a single-note idea in **bar 19**, notice how the flurry of eighth notes picks up the intensity of the solo. This lick, which has you skip strings to play intervals of 6ths, creates colorful motion in contrast to previous adjacent-string licks. In **bar 20**, the lick resolves with a simple B♭ Major Pentatonic lick. Use only a few choice notes to create a lick that really swings.

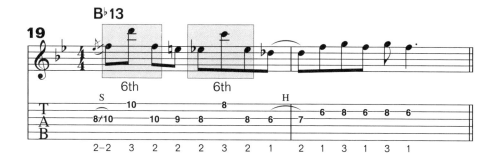

Chord tones are highlighted against the V chord in **bar 21**.

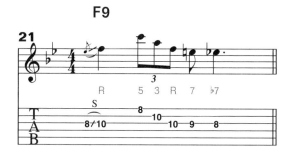

Double stops return in **bar 22**, keeping the fluctuation going between the single- and double-note phrases. This lick in 3rds moves chromatically from the root-3rd combination to the 3rd-5th combination.

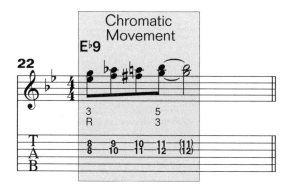

Summary

Jump blues has some jazz influences and is itself a precursor of rock 'n' roll. A motivic approach, where ideas recur throughout and are sequenced, will help create a unified solo. Chromatic movement in the lines, and the liberal use of chord and double-stop licks will earmark the style.

JAZZ BLUES

Blues has always influenced jazz, and over the years, more and more jazz seeps into the blues. In jazz blues, we find more extended chords—9th, 11th, and 13ths—and chords with alterations—min7(♭5), 7(♯9), and so on. This solo covers two 12-bar choruses of a jazz-blues progression in B♭.

With Solo, Track 26
Backing Track, Track 27

Two Jazzy

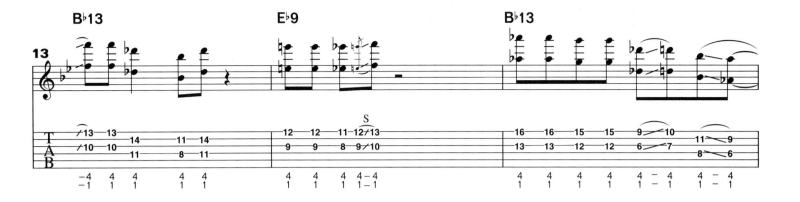

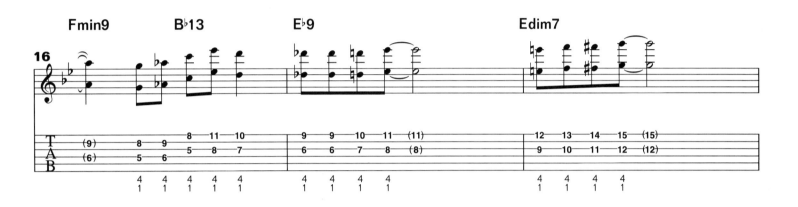

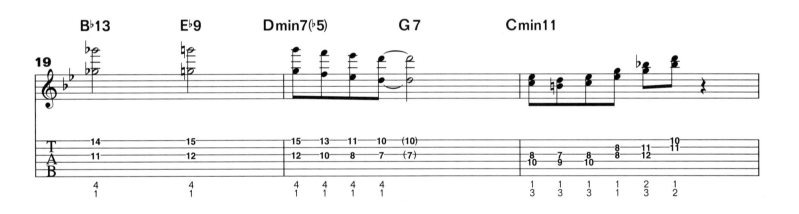

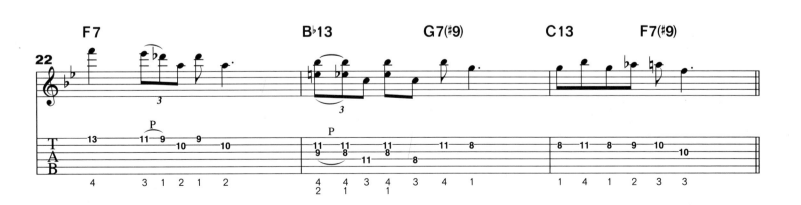

Analysis

In this style, there are a lot of chord changes. These are carefully outlined in the solo. In **bar 1**, there is a short chromatic motif contrasted by a string-skipping lick from the B♭ Major Pentatonic scale in 5th position. This is followed in **bar 2** by a return of the first motif, this time starting on G, over the quick-change IV chord (E♭9).

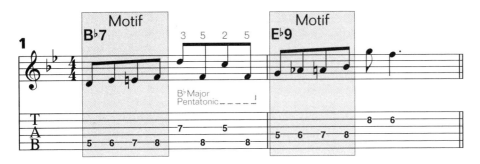

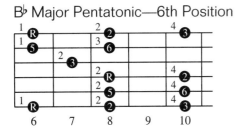

The Fmin9 chord in **bar 4** needs to lead strongly to the IV chord in **bar 5** in this style. The Fmin9 to B♭13 is a ii–V chord movement into the IV chord (E♭9), which is the quintessential jazz progression. These can be viewed as *secondary chords*; that is, they are the ii and the V of the IV. The use of a B Diminished 7th arpeggio over the B♭13 makes a strong melodic line because the B (enharmonically respelled C♭) is the ♭9th of the B♭13 chord, creating a jazzy harmonic tension. Jazz improvisation is all about *tension* (*dissonance*, clashing) and *release* (*resolution*, coming back to a harmonious sound).

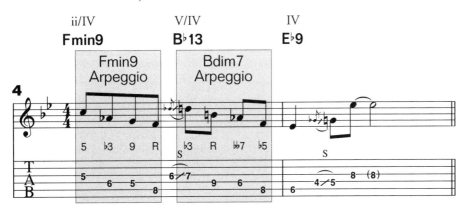

The simple resolution in **bar 6** to a consonant chord-tone lick balances the dissonance of **bars 4 and 5**. The tonality of the Edim7 chord (E–G–B♭–D♭) is outlined with chord tones. There is no need to use a lot of notes over a tense chord; a simple phrase works great.

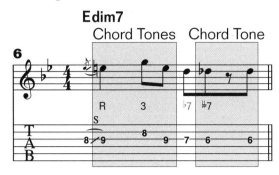

Bars 8–9 include another ii–V progression. A simple chromatic phrase, moving from the root (D) to the ♭3rd (F), gracefully covers the Dmin7(♭5) chord while the ♭9th (A♭) adds color to the G7. The phrase resolves simply with the ♭3rd and root of the Cmin11 chord.

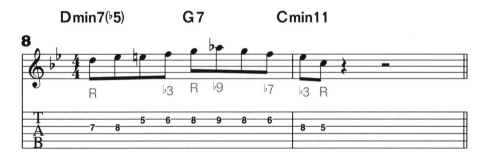

A *tritone substitution* occurs in **bar 10**. We use the dominant chord a tritone above the root (F)—in this case a B7 arpeggio (B–D♯–F♯–A). This works because the B7 chord includes the ♭7 (E♭/D♯), ♭5 (B/C♭), 3 (A), and the ♭9 (G♭/F♯) above an F root, providing tension over the V chord, F7. The tritone substitution is a very common device used in all styles of jazz to build the tension of a solo.

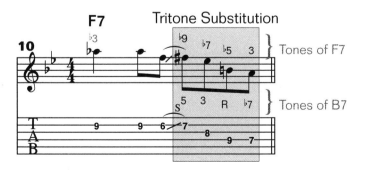

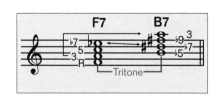

Starting in **bar 13**, the second chorus uses octaves (in double stops). This is another common jazz technique that is a very specific jazz sound and different than most blues devices. Once again, notice the simplicity of the licks; they are short three- and four-note licks that don't clutter the solo with unnecessary notes.

In **bars 17–18**, the octaves move in a concise chromatic fashion, mirroring the first motif presented in **bar 1**, over the E♭9 and the Edim7 chords. The return of this motif is both unifying and economic, as there are no wasted notes.

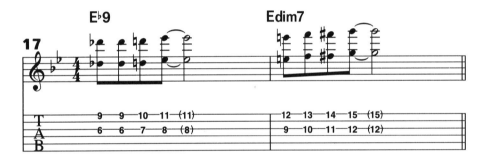

Bar 19 epitomizes the idea of simplicity and note economy.

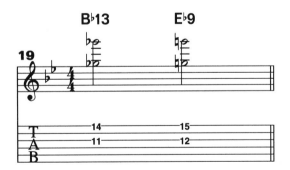

The notes of **bar 20** lay down a simple diatonic lick that resolves to the root (D) over the Dmin7($\flat$5) chord. This note is also the 5th of the next chord (G7), so let the pitch simply ring out for the rest of the measure. Some of the best notes are the ones you don't play.

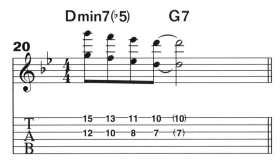

The lick in **bar 21** is a cool, double-stop pattern in 3rds that moves through the chord tones of the Cmin9 chord. It's a nice break from the preceding string of octave phrases.

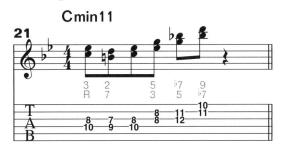

The turnaround of this chorus is a great place to play a more bluesy B$\flat$ Minor Pentatonic lick and just rock out. This provides a strident contrast to all the previous jazz-infused phrases.

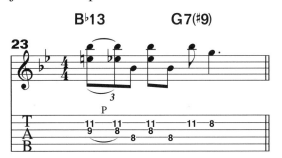

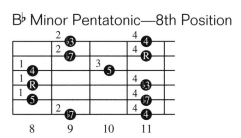

Summary

In the jazz-blues style, expect to find many harmonic devices borrowed from jazz. These will include lots of extended and altered chords, the use of secondary ii–V progressions and tritone substitutions. In your jazz-blues solos, experiment with jazz techniques, such as playing lines in octaves and superimposing arpeggios from one chord over another to highlight upper extensions and altered chord tones.

8-BAR SHUFFLE BLUES

While less common than the 12-bar blues, the 8-bar blues form is a standard as well. Perhaps the most famous 8-bar blues tune is Big Bill Broonzy's "Key to the Highway," which has been covered by such varied artists as Count Basie, Chuck Berry, Eric Clapton, John Lee Hooker, John Hammond, and Buddy Guy. This solo covers two 8-bar shuffle blues choruses in the key of A.

With Solo, Track 28
Backing Track, Track 29

Big Bill's Changes

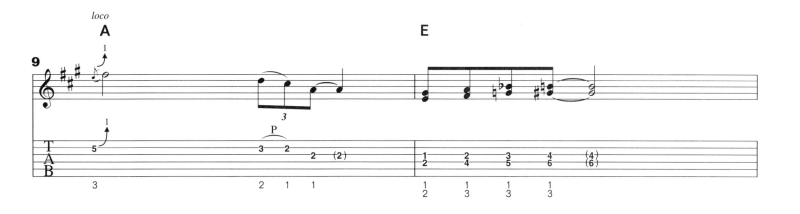

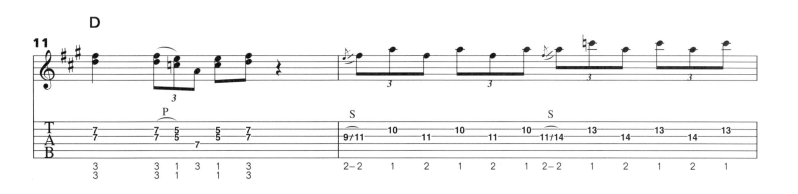

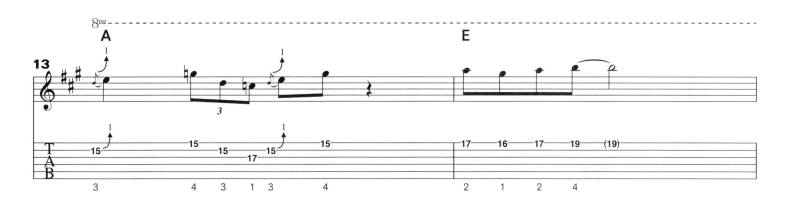

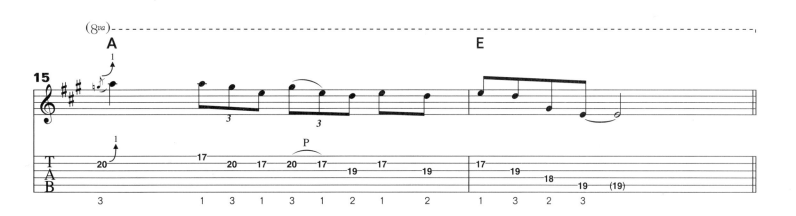

Analysis

In an 8-bar form, the chord changes move more rapidly than in the 12-bar form, therefore the solo should involve short musical phrases that define the rapidly changing harmonies. The appearance of the V chord in **bar 2** gives the 8-bar form a distinct personality of its own. After a basic bend into the root (A) in **bar 1**, the root (E) in **bar 2** is highlighted to accommodate the V chord (E). The bends in both bars add to the blues feel.

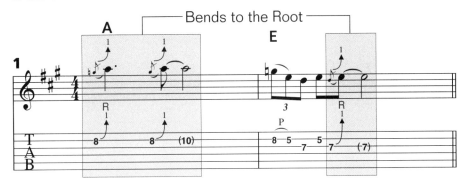

In **bar 3**, the A Minor Pentatonic scale continues to be the scale of choice, but notice how the root (D) and ♭7th (C) are given special attention over the IV chord (D).

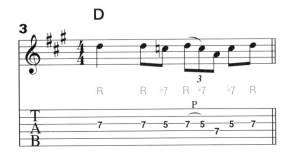

A Minor Pentatonic—5th Position

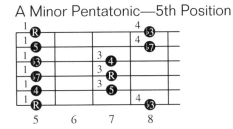

The energy of this chorus moves to a higher level here, propelled by the driving triplet figures throughout **bar 5**. Increasing the number of notes while at the same time repeating a rhythmic figure is a powerful way to build intensity. The combination of the A Minor Pentatonic scale with an added major 3rd (C♯) on the 9th fret of the 1st string creates a potent lick over the I chord (A).

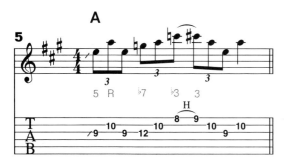

Bar 7 ascends to the upper register, which is a great place to peak the solo, especially after playing in lower registers in the previous bars. The rhythm continues to burn as the triplet idea is restated. Observe the simplicity of the lick: It consists of only three pitches. Once again, the fundamental principle of blues improvisation is the economic use of notes joined with a pulsating rhythm.

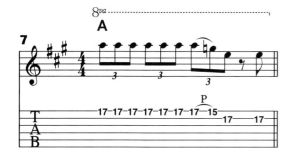

As the second 8-bar chorus commences in **bar 9**, a return to the lower register creates tonal contrast to the rousing finish of the first chorus. A simple A Major scale phrase offers a harmonic contrast to the A Minor Pentatonic scale and creates a subtle beginning to the new chorus.

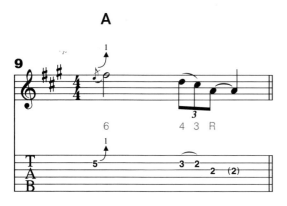

As the V chord (E) arrives in **bar 10**, the use of the double-stop 3rds beefs up the sound of this chorus after the understated single-note line in **bar 9**.

The continuation of the double-stop theme in **bar 11** maintains the energy of the solo. It is followed in **bar 12** by a lick in the higher register that is fueled by a repetitive triplet figure.

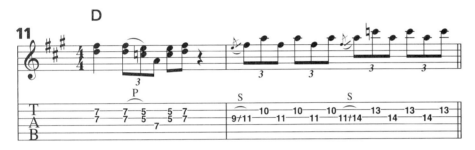

At this juncture of the solo, the notes proceed higher up the fretboard. This movement sets us up for the strong emotional climax in the coming bars. The two bends in **bar 13** begin this process.

The lick in **bar 14**, from an E Major scale, offers a nice contrast to the previous pentatonic licks and works well over the V chord (E).

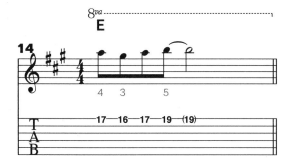

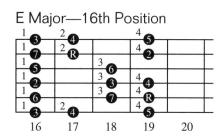

The chorus culminates in the home position of the A Minor Pentatonic scale at the 17th fret. The opening bend followed by the pull-off in **bar 15** brings the solo to a wailing conclusion, followed by a simple broken E7 chord in **bar 16.**

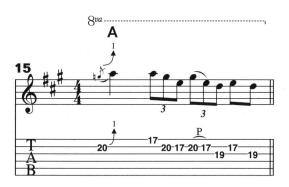

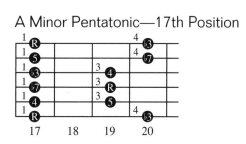

Summary

The 8-bar form is often played with swing 8ths. The chords change more rapidly than in the 12-bar form, so it is helpful to think in short phrases. Along with this, a sense of economy with your note choices and lots of energy will help you ride the pulsating rhythms of an 8-bar blues.

GOSPEL BLUES

There is a point where the sacred (gospel music) and the profane (blues, the devil's music) strike an uneasy alliance. The gospel-blues style uses the guitar's emotive possibilities to propel its lyrical, spiritual message. The Rev. Gary Davis (1896–1972) and Blind Willie Johnson (1902–1947) were key proponents of the style. This 8-bar gospel-blues solo uses a lot of triplets, emphasizing the swing feel.

With Solo, Track 30
Backing Track, Track 31

Preachin' the Blues

Analysis

The variety of chords in the gospel-blues style sets up a number of harmonic options for shaping a colorful solo. Double-stop licks are a great way to start a chorus in this style. This lick, over the I chord (B♭), is built from the B♭ Major Pentatonic scale.

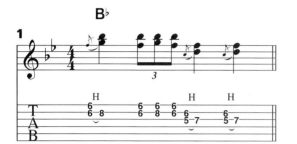

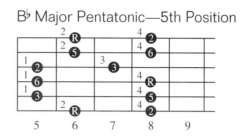

B♭ Major Pentatonic—5th Position

The bend to the unison (the note is played before and after we bend to it) of the root (D) over the III chord (D7) in **bar 2** exemplifies the simplicity of a good blues lick.

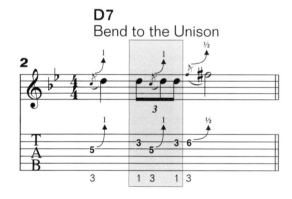

In **bar 3**, the repeating triplet rhythm combined with the repetitive melodic figure against the IV chord (E♭) lifts the energy of the solo.

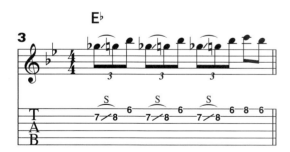

The best way to solo over the Edim7 chord in **bar 4** is to use an arpeggio.

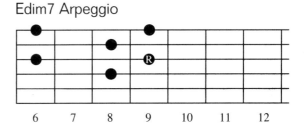

Following the basic Bᵇ Major Pentatonic lick in **bar 5** over the I chord (Bᵇ), the half-step bend to the F in **bar 6** accents the ᵇ7th of the VI chord (G7). This gives a subtle and soulful touch to the line.

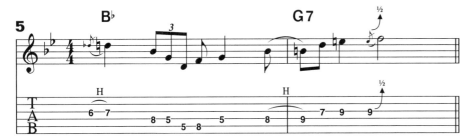

The double-stop 6ths, beginning in **bar 7** and finishing the solo in **bar 8**, outline the harmony of the II chord (C7), the V chord (F7) and the I chord (Bᵇ). The inclusion of an augmented V chord, FAug, at the end serves to provide a powerful pull back to the beginning of the progression so that the song can continue after the solo.

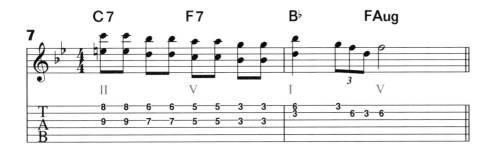

This solo covers one 8-bar chorus in the gospel-blues style. This solo, in contrast to "Preachin' the Blues" on page 88, uses a straight-8th feel.

With Solo, Track 32
Backing Track, Track 33

The Chapel of Blues

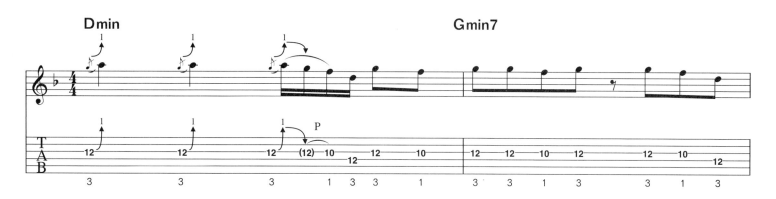

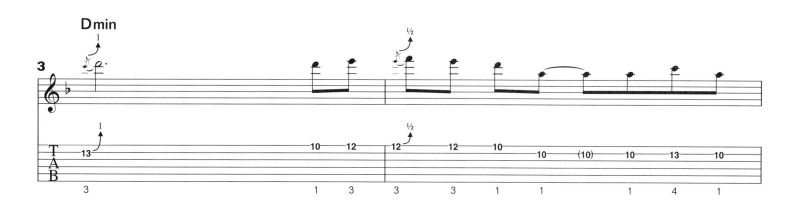

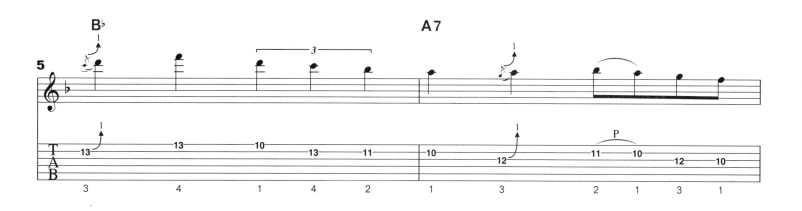

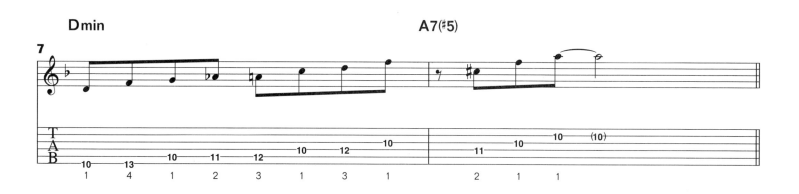

Analysis

This short minor blues solo features small pockets of notes that are rhythmically simple and capture the essence of the harmonic motion. In **bar 1**, the bends immediately lend a blues feel to this D Minor Pentatonic lick over the i chord (Dmin). **Bar 2** follows with notes from the same scale accenting the root (G) and ♭7th (F) against the iv chord (Gmin7).

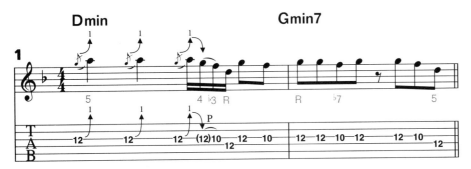

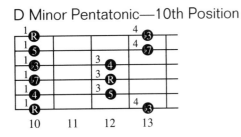

D Minor Pentatonic—10th Position

Bars 3–4 add the 2nd from the D Natural Minor scale to the D Minor Pentatonic scale. Notice the pause after the bend in **bar 3**. Let the emotional bend ring out to fortify the phrasing of the solo.

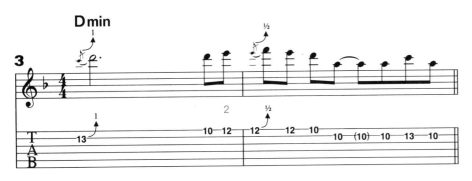

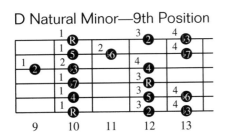

D Natural Minor—9th Position

In **bar 5**, VI (B♭) moves toward the V (A7) in **bar 6**. Use the notes of the D Natural Minor scale, accenting the chord tones (highlighted) of the B♭ and A7, to shape a strong, harmonically sound lick over these chords. The minor scale creates an even stronger melodic sense than the minor pentatonic scale.

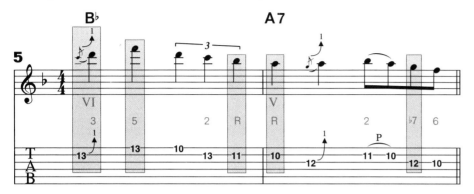

The flurry of eighth notes in **bar 7** ascends through the D Blues scale over the i chord (Dmin), returning the solo to its bluesy beginnings; this eighth-note run also propels the rhythmic intensity. The solo ends neatly in **bar 8** with an augmented (root–3rd–♯5th) arpeggio lick over the A7(♯5) turnaround chord. This chord has a strong need to resolve to the i chord (Dmin).

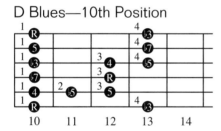

D Blues—10th Position

Summary

Gospel blues is a very emotional style, and your solos will benefit from the liberal use of the blues guitarist's ultimate heart-strings-pulling technique: bends. The inclusion of a variety of chord types in gospel-blues tunes, such as the diminished 7th and augmented (7♯5) chords, presents good opportunities for varying your note choices.

Conclusion

Congratulations. You have completed *Blues Soloing Strategies for Guitar*. Having studied a number of lead guitar solos in a variety of blues styles, you will be better prepared to create effective solos of your own. Learning the blues, however, is a life-long process, so keep studying. There is no substitute for listening to the greats, so check out as many recordings as possible and support live blues music wherever you can. The most important thing for you to do is get out there and play yourself. We'll see you on the bandstand!

SCALE GLOSSARY

The most commonly used scales for blues soloing are the blues scale, which is just a minor pentatonic scale with an added ♭5, and the major pentatonic scale. Most guitarists just learn a few "box patterns" for these scales, and as a result get stuck in them. While the one-position box patterns for these scales are useful, you should also try to think of them as complete scale systems that cover the entire fretboard. Keep in mind that any pattern is transposable by simply moving the root to the desired note. Learning your scales this way will give you far more freedom as a soloist.

A Blues Scale (A Minor Pentatonic)

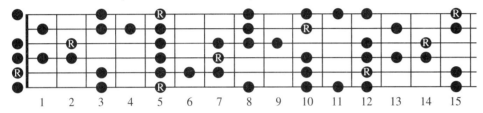

E Blues Scale (E Minor Pentatonic)

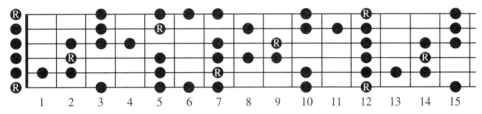

A Major Pentatonic Scale

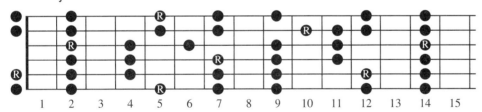

E Major Pentatonic Scale

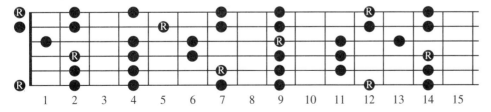

ARPEGGIO GLOSSARY

Here are some of the commonly used arpeggio patterns for playing blues solos. As
with any pattern without open strings, these are transposable to any root.

G7 Arpeggio

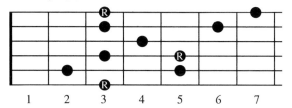

C#dim Arpeggio

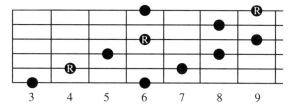

Amin7 Arpeggio

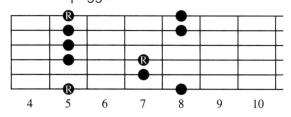

Dmin7(♭5) Arpeggio

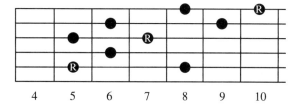

Emin7 Arpeggio

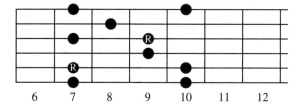

FAug Arpeggio

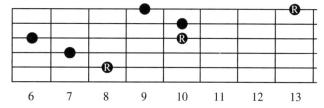

A Arpeggio

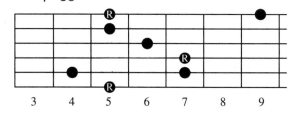

B♭6 Arpeggio

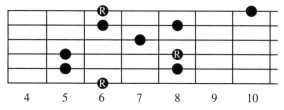